Bar and Restaurant Success

Nick Fosberg

Bar and Restaurant Success

Printed by:
90-Minute Books
302 Martinique Drive
Winter Haven, FL 33884
www.90minutebooks.com

Copyright © 2016, Nick Fosberg

Published in the United States of America

Book ID: 160713-00464

ISBN-13: 978-1945733017
ISBN-10: 1945733012

For more information on 90-Minute Books including finding out how you can publish your own lead
generating book, visit www.90minutebooks.com or call (863) 318-0464

Here's What's Inside...

Section 1:
The Truth & Myths Of Profitable Advertising

Chapter 1:
Introduction

If you're a bar, restaurant, pizzeria, or any other type of owner or operator in the food and beverage world and your goal is to make more money, attract more customers, and outsmart your competition, don't read this book; MEMORIZE it!

It reveals, in crystal-clear detail, a very powerful and profitable way to take your bar or restaurant business to the next level with the least amount of risk to your marketing dollars. This book will change the way you market your business for the rest of your life. It will give you the biggest advantage you've ever had over your competition and the opportunity to create $5,000, $10,000, $20,000, or more in additional sales with literally ZERO risk to your marketing dollars.

This book will do all this for you by giving you a step-by-step, proven marketing and promotional system that has been used by myself and hundreds of other operators around the country to add over $100,000 in sales in less than 12 months' time. This system is responsible for creating the highest-grossing online promotions—$59,625 to be exact—in the history of the bar and restaurant business with zero marketing expenses.

Learn this system, and you'll never have to worry about a promotion failing. How is that possible? Because you'll know exactly how to determine if your new promotion will be a success or a failure _before_ you even run it! You'll know what marketing channels will work, which ones won't, and what offers will bring you the most money.

Imagine having a crystal ball and being able to see into the future. That's the power you'll have once you learn this simple marketing and promotional system. It's that powerful!

What you're about to learn is an entirely NEW way to attract and retain customers with marketing messages that will make your brand stand out from all the others and instantly build trust and credibility with your customers.

By learning this system—and it can easily be learned—you can expect immediate benefits:

- Exactly what to say in your marketing messages to get customers to take action and walk in your doors
- How to get new customers to do business with you before they ever think of going to your competitors
- How to easily get 50 to 100 customers to take you up on your offers and how to do that with zero marketing costs
- More profits than ever before (as long as your food and beverage costs stay the same)
- The three fastest ways to grow your business working for you 24/7 on autopilot, which will leverage your time and resources
- Knowledge of the most powerful secret of all: how to get your customers to feel like they know you on a personal level through your marketing messages, even if they've never met you before!

Anyone, including you, can read this book in a matter of an hour or so. It will be a very exciting read because every five to ten minutes another light bulb will go off in your head, generating new ideas and strategies that are so simple for you to implement and profit from immediately!

By this time tomorrow, you'll know exactly how I help my clients get hundreds of new customers in their doors in less than 30 days. You'll be able to put this same strategy in place tomorrow and see new customers within days. However, I don't suggest reading this book just one time. I recommend that you reread it several times. Memorize it. With each reading, you'll get more ideas and new secrets to give you the success and freedom that you're after!

If you have a manager who does your marketing, make it a priority for them to read this and give you the cliff notes on it. Have them write out the step-by-step marketing and promotional system I'm going to give you and what their first set of plans are to put it into action. If you're paying them to grow your business, there's a little homework that goes along with you paying them good money!

In the next year or two, you will start to see other consultants in our industry teaching this system as if it were their own. There's nothing I can do about that, but do I care? Not really. What I care about is getting this system and these strategies into the hands of every bar and restaurant operator in the country because of the impact it will have on their lives, their businesses, and their customers.

How This System Was Born

Let me introduce myself and reveal how this system was born. My name is Nick Fosberg, and at the time I'm writing this book, I own two bars in the Rockford, IL area. Before I go on, it's important for me to point out that Forbes Magazine just recently ranked Rockford, IL as the third worst place to live in in the United States, so you're probably in a better position than I ever was to grow your business as fast as possible! With that said, if what you're going to discover in this book will work for me, in the economy I'm faced with, it'll work for you too!

I grew up in the bar business my entire life. I remember watching my dad count stacks of cash in his off office, at one of his bars, The Rusty Nail. I remember seeing my dad buying drinks for the entire bar and customers thanking him. It seemed like "fun" work. At a very young age, I knew I'd follow in his footsteps.

When I was 24, my dad gave me the opportunity to buy one of his bars. Then things got interesting and not so "fun." Because I'd grown up in the business and my dad was very successful, I thought I knew everything, but I was wrong!

Six to eight months into owning my own bar, I was very close to going out of business. I blamed it on the bad economy and new competition in my area, but was it really that? No. That was an excuse I was telling myself because I thought that I was doing things right when I wasn't.

Suddenly I found myself paying bills out of my own pocket to keep the place running. This was my wake-up call, and ***it was the best thing that ever happened to me.***

I knew that getting more new customers in the door and getting existing customers to come back more often was the only thing that could bring my bar back to life. I went to our trade magazines and websites for help but came up short for answers. It was all very generic information. I couldn't find anything on how to attract and retain customers in a step-by-step format.

I did research on the Internet, bought marketing courses and books, and went to marketing seminars to help me find the answers I was looking for. I became so intrigued by what I was learning that I literally became a marketing junkie! It got so bad that my wife would yell at me to put the damn books down and get my face out of the computer screen. But I couldn't stop! I was addicted!

After just three months of studying new business growth strategies, I started to implement what I was learning. It was tough at first because all of it was kind of like a foreign language, but it worked. I slowly saw a positive response from my marketing: new customers coming in the doors and repeat visits.

Then one day changed my life and career forever. I decided to invest $8,000 into a one-day consultation with my marketing coach. I flew out to Atlanta to see him and put a marketing and promotional plan in place. I remember Dave asking me when I got there, *"What can we do that makes you the most money in the shortest amount of time?"*

I laughed and said, *"Dave, I just paid you $8,000, not including travel fees to come out here for you to give me that answer!"*

Dave replied, *"Nick, I don't I understand the bar and restaurant business. I need you to help me understand all the different ways you go about generating cash flow. Then I can help map out a plan to get you to where you really want to be and increase that cash flow!"*

I felt much better after that answer. It took me a while to come up with a response, but then that light bulb went off in my head. The answer was parties and group events.

I remembered that when someone had a birthday party or event at my bar, it sometimes brought in 40 to 60 people. Most of them were new customers, and they drank like fish!

Dave said, *"That's our focus. We need to figure out how to book more parties and group events because it creates big paydays for you and brings in a ton of new customers. If you do a good job at providing good service, there's no reason we can't get any of those new customers to come back!"*

During my day with Dave, we created a few different systems and strategies to attract new customers but also to book as many parties as I could. One of the first things we did was write a "sales" letter and sent it out to 300 businesses in my area with an offer they couldn't refuse for office holiday parties.

Within 2 days of sending the mailing out, I had booked 13 parties, and 40 to 50 people came to each party. That brought in over 800 customers total, and it only cost me around $300 to do the mailing. The average check for each person was close to $20. That's $16,000 in sales from a $300 investment. To be exact, my sales from this one promotion were $16,091!

That's when I realized that this is where the money is and that this new marketing stuff really works! Over the next several months, I tried different marketing strategies to book events and parties. Through a little trial and error, I finally created a proven system to get groups of 30 to 50 to 75 people in my doors, 1 to 3 times every single week, even during the traditionally slow times of the year—without spending a dime on advertising.

My sales doubled. I quit using radio, TV, and newspaper advertising as my main sources of advertising, which saved me anywhere from $1,000 to $2,000 a month. I was also bringing hundreds of new faces into my bar.

Important

This book isn't all about booking parties and events, all though it is one of the strategies I will talk about, so if you're concerned that you don't have the space or room or business model to book parties, don't worry. This is just one of the many profitable strategies I'll talk about deeper into in the book.

How Bar Restaurant Success Was Born

After my success, my coach gave me the idea to start teaching the systems and strategies we created to other owners outside my area because. That's when I started my own coaching and consulting business, Bar Restaurant Success.

Today, I spend 99% of my working time on Bar Restaurant Success and about 1% of my time on both bars. Luckily, I've figured out how to systematize the bar/restaurant businesses to the point that they run themselves. Right now most of what I do is look over reports and numbers and have a weekly meeting with my mangers to go over new promotions and in-house systems that need to be tweaked.

I've created a 12-month marketing and promotional calendar and membership area for my managers with all the promotions that have worked over the last 8 years. Inside the members' area are training videos and marketing templates that my managers use to market and run the events. I'll talk more about this later, but it's what I give our Bar Restaurant Success Elite members access to for their own managers to use and implement.

Systematizing my other businesses allows me to do what I love most: spend time with my wife and kids and help owners, operators, and managers like yourself to take their bar/restaurant businesses to the next level. There's no greater feeling in the world than being able to provide value to someone else and make a positive impact, not only on their business but in their life, financially and emotionally.

> "Anyone who stops learning is old, whether at twenty or eighty. Anyone who keeps learning stays young."
> **– Henry Ford**

I continue to spend $30,000 or more every year on my own education. I buy and read at least two books per month on business, marketing, leadership, and productivity. I have two different marketing coaches who help me with my goals in different parts of my businesses. I'm part of a $15,000-a-year mastermind group, where I meet with 20 other successful business owners three times a year to help each other grow our businesses with different strategies. With that said, I practice what I preach, and I'm always looking for new strategies and techniques to test and then bring them to our industry.

It's important to understand that there's always room to learn more. Becoming successful is a never-ending process. When you stop learning, when you lose the hunger to keep on moving forward, business and life come to a standstill. Don't expect growth in business and in life when you do nothing to make that happen. You have to keep the hunger and motivation going. When you do, you'll get everything you want out of your business, which will give you the lifestyle you want.

How This Book Is Laid Out & What to Expect

This book is laid out into four sections that will walk you step-by-step through the fastest, easiest, least risky way to grow your bar/restaurant business with minimal effort.

Section One: Set Yourself Up for Success

This entire book means nothing to you if you don't believe in every ounce of information that is revealed in Section One. This is where I break down the truth about what business we are really in, the myths about marketing and advertising, why most owners struggle to get a positive return on their marketing dollars, and how to fix that.

Section One is about $100,000 worth of coaching and learning through trial and error over the past eight years in this business. What you'll get here isn't just what I believe about business growth, but what is preached and taught by the most advanced and highest-paid marketing and promotional consultants on the planet.

At the end of Section One, I also cover the five key ingredients you need in every advertisement that you do in order to get the highest ROI on your marketing dollars. Without any of the five key ingredients, you're almost guaranteed to lose money.

Section Two: LRVO Formula & Winning Over New Customers

In Section Two, I reveal my Loyal Regular Value Optimization (LRVO) system. This is the formula I use to attract and retain new customers. It's the same formula I use to create up to $30,000 or more in sales for my clients with zero marketing expenses.

I invited Mike Ganino, an expert in branding, company culture, and creating winning strategies for turning new customers into raving fans, to talk about how to get your staff to give your customers the best service and the best experience possible, so they tell everyone they know about your business.

I brought Mike in on this because I can give you the easiest and fastest way to get new customers in the doors, but, the truth is, if they don't have good experiences, they won't be back, which means that everything else you did to acquire those customers becomes worthless.

Section Three: Big-Money Promotions & Profitable Marketing Strategies

This is the most exciting section of all, but _don't_ go skipping right to it. I laid this book out in the order it takes to make big-money promotions a huge success for you. Section Two means nothing to you if you don't understand and believe in Section One. Section three **WON'T** work without section two being applied, so don't try to take a shortcut because if you do, that shortcut will actually lead you down the wrong path and make things harder for you.

What you'll discover in Section Three is:

- How to easily create $5,000 to $10,000 or more in sales, with zero marketing expenses
- How to know whether a promotion will be a success or a failure before you ever run it
- Multiple promotional ideas that you can easily start using to generate some quick sales and pack a slow week night
- So much more

Section Four: Your Step By Step Guide To Doubling Your Loyal Customers In The Fastest & Least Riskiest Way

In Section Four, I walk you step-by-step through the marketing and promotional system I have set up in both of my bars, which is the same exact system I set up for all my clients.

I hold nothing back here. When I considered putting this book together, I thought to myself "What is the one thing I can put into this book that will give the most value to my reader, if implemented?" This is it: You don't have to pay $8,000 to $10,000 to meet with a marketing consultant to figure out how to put a system in place for attracting and retaining new customers; you're going to get everything you need, step-by-step, right here.

I also give you four simple blueprints that you can follow using this system to make $50,000 in extra sales within 12 months or fewer.

Without action, nothing will happen, and reading this book will be a waste of your time. I dedicated this section to getting you motivated enough to start putting this to work in your business today, rather than tomorrow.

I'm always reading self-improvement books to keep myself going and to keep the energy and huger going. We are all human, and we all lose our drive at different times in our lives. By reading something motivational, you start thinking about the next level in your business and in your life. It brings that drive and hunger back.

This chapter is meant to make you feel unstoppable and to give you the opportunity to get cracking on this right away by doing it yourself, or having it all done for you. Some owners love to learn and figure things out on their own. They treat this like a puzzle and do great with it. Some just want things done for them because they have enough on their plates, and they don't want to create more work for themselves.

Section Four is meant to help whichever owner you are get on the fastest path to success and creating multi-thousand-dollar promotions with the least amount of risk to your pocket book.

The book you're holding right now represents a tiny investment compared to what you will earn by applying what it is you're about to learn. It's now up to you! All you have to do to turn this tiny benefit into a financial windfall is read on! Get rid of all the distractions, pay attention to what you're reading, and do it with an open mind. Then put this into action.

And that will be easy to do. You'll see what I mean as you continue through the book.

Chapter 2:
What Business We Are Really In

This book's primary focus is on attracting and retaining new customers through marketing and promotional strategies; how to boost your sales with the least amount of risk to your pocket book.

However, I don't want to mislead you in any way by making you think that all you need to do is apply the marketing strategies in this book to become a huge success. That's far from the truth.

Your number one priority should always be customer satisfaction. We are in the hospitality business. People visit our bars and restaurants to not only eat and drink but to have great experiences.

You can serve the best dishes in the world, but if your server disrespects your customer, if they provide a horrible experience, that customer will go somewhere else. The "lead magnet" strategy I cover in Section Two is the easiest and fastest way to attract new customers, but those new customers won't be back, and all of your marketing efforts will be a waste, unless they have good experiences.

When I became a marketing junkie and started to see my business grow, I totally took customer service off my radar. I focused 100% of my energy on marketing and promotions because I was having such a fun time seeing my marketing and promotions finally work! That was a big mistake.

It wasn't until I read Jon Taffer's book *Raise the Bar* that I realized the **customer's experience is more important than anything else.** I got so caught up in the cash flow and the excitement of creating advertising that was finally working that I didn't realize I was draining my pocket book.

I don't want that to happen to you, and I don't want to mislead you or have you thinking that I believe all you need is great marketing and promotions. Giving the customer the best experience still trumps everything else in this business; however, if you want to build your business in the <u>fastest</u> way possible, **that does come down to marketing & promotions!**

Before I go into the gold of this book, it's important for you to know and understand what advertising really is, what most owners are currently doing, and why they see very little (if any) ROI on their marketing dollars.

The Truth About Advertising That Most Owners Forget & Why This Is Critical to Your Success

Studies show that we see or hear over 5,000 marketing messages a day, and we avoid 99% of them like the plague. We can now listen to our favorite music without commercials for a few bucks a month. We can get all of our favorite news headlines without ads right on our phones and tablets. We can watch all of our favorite shows while skimming past commercials.

Do you see where this is going? Do you see what the future holds for us? It's getting harder and harder to get our marketing messages in front of customers because they now have the opportunity to eliminate MOST of the marketing messages being sent to them. And it's only going to **_keep_** getting harder as years go on!

To add to that, there's more competition than ever before, fighting for our customers' attention and business. Lucky for you, after reading this book and understanding the sole purpose of advertising, **you won't ever have this problem.**

Right now I'm going to reveal to you the most important thing you could ever learn about marketing and advertising.

Remember this one thing for the rest of your career in this business, or any business, and you'll get three times the results on your marketing dollars.

What Most Bar/Restaurant Owners Do When Advertising Their Businesses

When I talk to a new private client or am critiquing a marketing piece for a member of Bar Restaurant Success, I see exactly what I used to do when I almost lost my bar. I call it "image" or "awareness" advertising, where you have a fancy ad with a picture, your logo really large at the top, all of your contact information, and the price(s) of whatever it is you're promoting.

Here's what's wrong with this type of advertising:

1. You can't track or measure your results because if someone were to see that ad on social media, in the newspaper, or somewhere else, you would have no clue where that customer came from, meaning you would have no clue if that ad made you money or put a deep hole in your pocket book.

2. You look just like your competition because this is what 99% of owners do.

How do you stand out? Remember, people tune out marketing messages because they are bombarded with over 5,000 of them every day.

Keep in mind that I'm referring to PAID advertising. Posting your food and drink specials on social media is great; you should do that. Anytime *you're spending money*, you should try to get your customers to take action in a way that _you can track and measure the results._

I'll get into much more detail on this as we go further into the book. Right now I just want to set the frame and open your mind up to the sole purpose of advertising.

What Is Advertising?

What is the purpose of advertising? As I learned from reading well over 50 marketing books, advertising is "multiplied *salesmanship.*" Did you hear that? **SALESMENSHIP!** It has one purpose and one purpose only: *to make a sale.* **Not to win awards for how great it looks.** It's to put <u>money in your registers.</u>

Some owners and operators are infected with the "branding" disease. That's the type of branding you see all the big corporations do. They put their logo and image advertising all over the place without any clue about how much product they really sold with those millions of dollars in ads.

Your brand is very important, but you can still gain "awareness" and you can still "brand" your bar or restaurant business with advertising that is ***DESIGNED*** *to* ***SELL***, that is designed to get your customer to take action on your offer. By doing this, you'll make more money, you'll *know* whether you're making money or losing money on your advertising, and you'll get the same amount of branding but in a more positive and powerful way! (You'll see what I mean in Section 3.)

What You Can Learn
From A Fisherman

I want to tell you a quick story about a fisherman, Captain John Rade, and his greatest secret to catching fish, which has everything to do with us catching new and existing customers for our promotions and offers.

Captain John is from the Long Island area, and to understand how great a fisherman he is, you should know that government agencies regulate fishing. For sports anglers, the number of fish you can catch is low. Commercial fishermen, who earn a living from the sea, have much higher limits. Captain John is a commercial fisherman who specializes in catching fish for a living to sell to restaurants and fish markets, but he's a rare type of commercial fisherman, a "Pinhooker". This means that he doesn't rely on the usual commercial-fishing methods; no big nets and no long lines with hundreds of bait hooks.

He just goes out in his motorboat with a rod and reel and hooks his fish one at a time. Yet he always comes back with hundreds of pounds of fish. On a typical Saturday, The Viking Starship, a big party boat, takes out 50 to 60 fishermen. Captain John Rade usually out-fishes these 50 to 60 fishermen combined, fishing from the same waters.

A local newspaper reporter asked him, *"How do you do this? How are you able to out-fish 50 to 60 others in the same waters, by yourself, time and time again?"*

This Is How You MUST Think To
Profit from Your Advertising!

Captain John Rade's response is extremely critical to your success in marketing your bar or restaurant. He said to the reporter, *"Don't think like a fisherman; think like a fish!"*

"When most fishermen go out to fish, they think like fishermen. When I go out, I think like a fish." He devoted his life to this.

How often do you think like an owner, like a promoter, like a marketer? How little do you think like your target audience, who you're trying get to spend money with you?

Captain Rade said most fisherman go out and buy new shiny lures and colored, fancy gimmicks, but most of that stuff is designed to catch fishermen, not fish. Fishermen are always after new devices, and it's a waste of money because that's not what the fish want.

The Secret...

Captain Rade doesn't go after the stuff that catches fishermen. Instead, he studies everything there is to know about the fish he wants to catch: when they are hungry, what they like to eat as the seasons change, what bait runs in the water and attracts them on any given day. The most important thing he studies is the ocean, the environment his fish swim in. Why? Because the ocean affects his target more than anything else.

By studying all of this, knowing what bait to use and when and what the environment is like at all times, Captain Rade is able to out-fish everyone else because he knows what the *fish are after and when they will bite.*

The Questions You Need To Ask Yourself Before You Ever Write Another Check To Your Ad Rep

Before you spend another penny on marketing, think of who you're trying to catch and where you're going to catch them. Remember, people are always avoiding marketing messages, so the question is: How do we get in front of them, and when we do, how do we get them to pay the slightest bit of attention to our ads?

Then the question is: How do we get that potential customer to do what we want? How do we get them to come in our doors and spend money? Here's a little secret from the great philosopher Plato:

> "There's <u>only</u> 2 ways to get someone to do what you want. Either by force or persuasion."

What are we doing when we advertise our businesses? What are we doing when we promote our businesses? We are ***ASKING*** people to do business with us. The truth is, there are only two ways to get people to do what you ASK of them: exactly what Plato said, force or persuasion.

We can't use force, so we must use the art of persuasion and allow our reasoning to be accepted—or not—by others. That said, your advertising today ***MUST*** be ***persuasive***, and slapping your logo, food images, a fancy design, and prices on it doesn't cut it today. You must explain within your advertising how a customer will <u>benefit</u>, why you are making the offer, why they need to act now, what they will miss out on if they don't come, etc.

Conclusion

If you want average or poor results, then advertise like your competition. If you want to stand out and make money from your marketing, start focusing on strategy and your customer.

What is your goal? What promotion or offer are you going to use to reach that goal? Who is the best type of customer who will come in for your offer or promotion? Where is the best place to put your marketing message, so your best type of customer will see or hear it? What are you going to say to PERSUADE that customer that your offer or promotion is a better alternative to anything else they have available to them? Finally, how will you track and measure the results of your marketing?

Let's dive into the next chapter on how to make your advertising more persuasive. This will likely be one of the most valuable chapters of the book and a chapter you should re-read several times.

Chapter 3:
Why People Buy

How to Make Your Marketing Messages Persuasive & Get Customers To Take Action On Your Offers & Promotions

I'm going to let you in on an advanced secret that nobody talks about in our industry. If you master this, **you'll have a way to print your own money.** When I became a marketing junkie, I studied the psychology of **why people buy and how people come to a buying decision.**

Why did I do this?

If I knew the reasons that people come to buying decisions, then I'd know exactly what to say in my marketing to get new and existing customers to take me up on my offers and promotions. (Think like a fish.)

I discovered that people buy products and services *based on their emotions.* I discovered that if you can tell them how your offer or promotion will benefit them in some way, it will skyrocket the response of your marketing. It MUST benefit them! If not, why should they do what you're ASKING them to do, which is ultimately stepping foot through your doors for your offer.

The questions that everyone has when they see an ad or promotion are: What's in it for me? How is this going to benefit me? Why should I do business with you over your competition?

The marketing message that presents your offer or promotion must explain to your new or existing customers how they will benefit from what you're offering. If you can do this, you'll create pay days like the clients you'll hear about later in this book.

Before you ever send out an email or a direct mail piece, you need to get into the mind of your customer and think of them saying to themselves, *"Why should I take advantage of this?"* Then give them as many answers as you can think of, all within your marketing. This is also called "reason why" copy/marketing.

Example Of Trying To Persuade Someone To Come For Entertainment

Let's say that you're advertising a band. The thoughts in people's minds might be, *"Oh, this sounds like fun, but I gotta do xyz,"* or, *"I can't because I have my kids that night...."*

Now you have to think of what you can say in your marketing messages to overcome all of the objections that your audience could come up with.

You could say something like this:

"We all live very stressful lives. We deal with that pinhead boss on a day-to-day basis, so we owe it to ourselves to relieve some stress, to get out the house and have a good time. When you come to see BAND NAME, not only are you going to forget about the everyday BS, but you're going to be around a bunch of fun, outgoing people.

You're going to have a great time, one that is well deserved. Maybe you have kids? I've got kids too. I love them to death, but, man, sometimes I need a break. I'm sure you do too! Call up the grandparents, and get them lined up so you know your kids are taken care of while you're out having a good time."

That's just a quick example, but your new or existing customer will start saying to themselves, *"You're right! I haven't been out in a while, and I am stressed out. I need to relieve that stress and have a fun night out with the guys or the girls."*

In this business, some people need excuses to go out. I'm not saying that you should create excuses in all of your marketing, but it fits for this situation.

Think about St. Patrick's Day. Millions of people go out to party and have a good time. They call out of work; they get their kids taken care of. How many of them are Irish? A very small percentage! How many of them really know what St. Patrick's Day is all about? An even smaller percent!

Why do millions of non-Irish people, who don't know what St. Patrick's Day is about, go out and have a good time at bars and restaurants? Because it's an **_EXCUSE_** to go out, have fun, and spend money!

What you're trying to do is persuade customers to come in for your offer or promotion by explaining how they will benefit. Once they see how they will benefit, they have an excuse to take the fun/entertaining route rather than the usual boring route.

Example Of How To Persuade New Or Existing Customers In For A Food Promo

Let's say you are promoting a new steak dinner night. The question in your customer's or prospect's mind when they see your promotion might be: _"Why should I come in for this $15 steak dinner? How am I going to benefit from it? Why shouldn't I go to the big, corporate, chain steakhouse down the street?"_

Within my marketing message, I would respond by saying something like, _"You should come in because it's only $15, and everywhere else you'd pay $20 or more. Still, the price is just a bonus. When you come to ABC Bar & Grill we will cater to you, provide you with great service, and you won't have to worry about all of the clean-up."_

"Eating at home gets old, doesn't it? It takes you 20 minutes to prepare the food, 15 to 20 minutes to cook it, and another 15 minutes to clean up. It's a long, tiring process."

"Imagine this: You drive 5 minutes to ABC Bar & Grill, you sit down at a table—or the bar, if you prefer—order your food, have a cocktail, and sit back and relax. Within 10 to 15 minutes, your food is delivered to you hot and fresh, and then we clean up after you."

"So what do you say? Doesn't this seem much more relaxing, easier, and worth every penny?"

Do you see what I'm doing here? I'm painting a picture in the customer's head of how my offer will solve a problem they could be facing (not wanting to prep, cook, clean up) and how my offer will benefit them! This persuades them that my offer is a ***better*** alternative to anything else they could be doing.

Instead of releasing an ad with a steak image, my logo, the price tag, and my business info, I use compelling, persuasive copy that hits emotional triggers in my customers' minds that get them to justify taking advantage of my offer as their best alternative. I can still use a nice steak image, and I can still focus on branding with this type of marketing in a much more powerful and profitable way.

My goal in Section One of this book is to get you to understand the sole purpose of advertising and why traditional "branding/awareness" marketing ends up costing you money, rather than making you money.

Ask This Before Every Ad / Promo You Create!
"What Are You Really Selling???"

Here's one last golden nugget for you.

Before you ever run any ad or promotion, you need to ask yourself this question: *"What am I really selling?"*
Here are examples of other types of businesses to give you a better idea of what I mean:

Lawn care: You're not selling grass seed; *you're selling a greener lawn.*

Heating business: You're not selling boilers and BTUs; you're selling warmer, cozier winter nights at a 27% fuel savings.

Here's one of my favorites, one that I think is ingenious: The Marlboro man commercials weren't selling cigarettes; *they were selling the cooler image—the cool cowboy on a horse.*

What made that cool image of the cowboy? **The cigarette. Their product!**

What was the outcome? Marlboro became, and still is to this day, the number-one-selling cigarette brand.

What I used to do, and what I see every bar/restaurant owner doing, is focus on marketing food and drinks.

The real reason people are buying these products and services is the OUTCOME they will get FROM the products or services, the benefits they receive, the EXPERIENCES they will have!

What is it that you are selling?

You are **NOT** selling food.
You are **NOT** selling alcohol.

You are selling the benefits that customers will get from what you have to offer. If what you have to offer doesn't benefit your customer, or if they don't see the benefit of your offer or

promotion, ___your marketing will end up costing you money___
___rather than making you money.___

Conclusion

I'm hoping I've reached my goal at this point and am getting
you to agree with me that the "awareness" style of marketing
and advertising isn't going to get you the results you want, and
it's not going to set you apart from the competition. This style
of marketing will get you ignored because people are hit with
over 5,000 "awareness"-style marketing messages a day, which
they tune out.

The ultimate goal you're trying to achieve when spending your
own money on advertising your business is to get someone to
hand you money, so you make a profit and cover the costs of
your advertising. In order to do this effectively, it's all about
salesmanship!

Salesmanship means you must ___persuade___ your potential
customer on why your promotion is a better option then any
alternative they could think of and how they will benefit.
Benefiting doesn't always mean they get a discount. They can
benefit from the experience they have and actually pay a
premium price for it, so don't think that discounting is the only
way to benefit a customer.

Let's dive into the next chapter and go through the five key
ingredients you must have in every ad in order to get the
highest ROI on your marketing dollars. This chapter will also
help you understand more about how to craft each of your
persuasive marketing messages in a simple, step-by-step
format.

Chapter 4:
The Five Key Ingredients You Must Have In Your Marketing In Order To Get The Highest ROI On Your Advertising Dollars

Anytime you write an email, a social media post, a newspaper ad, or any type of paid media, you should have all five of these key ingredients in your marketing in order to get the highest ROI on your marketing dollars.

#1: A Powerful Headline

Your headline is the most important part of any ad that you create. You only have five seconds to catch the attention of your prospect. If you don't grab their attention, your marketing message doesn't stand a chance of being read, heard, or viewed.

> "Ninety percent of your marketing success will come from your headline!"

It's been said that an average of five times as many people read headlines than the copy. That means that if your headline doesn't grab their attention, you're wasting 90% of the money you spent on your marketing campaign.

When you're reading the paper or a magazine, what makes you stop and read certain articles? An eye-catching headline that interests you! That's what you need to create when you are sending your customers or new prospects an offer. You need to grab their attention and get them to say, *"I have to read this!"* or, *"This is interesting!"* You can have the best letter, ad, social media post, or email in world, but if you have a crappy headline, forget about it! It won't get read, opened, or viewed.

When it comes to writing email promotions, the headline is the subject line of your email. When you open emails, the ones that grab your attention are probably those with interesting subject lines. If you can tell the e-mail is another advertising campaign or a topic you have no interest in, chances are you don't open it.

What do you want as your headline? Let me tell you what you **DON'T** want, even though it's exactly what I used to do before I became a marketing junkie. _You don't want your logo or business name as your headline!_ This is what I see most owners do because they copy "brand awareness" advertising that every huge, corporate business does. Their sole focus is their image; it's focused on them, **NOT** the wants and desires of the prospects with whom they want to do business!

Let me give you some examples of proven headlines that pull huge results for anyone in the bar/restaurant business.

Why "Your Biz Name Here" Is Giving You & 99 Others A Free Meal

This headline is a benefit-driven headline as well as a curiosity-driven headline. Someone reads this and instantly thinks, _"I want a free meal! This interests me."_ Then they think, _"Why is this business giving me and 99 others free meals? I should read more and find out why and how I get mine!"_

(First Name), How Would You Like to Have a Beer with the Hottest Staff in (Your Town/City)?

You would use this in a mailer or social media post targeting single males or females, whichever works best for the goals you're after. I've used this headline on a postcard with a photo of staff on the front and this headline at the top. On the backside I put the same headline at the top as well. The reason for that is sometimes people see the backside of a postcard first, and you want to grab their attention instantly.

You could buy a mailing list of single men from 21 to 35 years old, who live within five miles of your business and send this postcard directly to their mailboxes. Tell me what single guy you know who wouldn't read the rest of this postcard after starting with a headline like this, especially if you really do have an attractive staff at your bar?

Local Restaurant Owner Infuriates The Big Chain Restaurants By Giving Away Hundreds Of Free Dinners

This is a curiosity-, news-driven headline that I've used in the newspaper and in direct mail. The marketing message told a story in the third person, as if a newspaper reporter wrote it, about how I was giving away free meals to get new customers in the door because it was so hard to compete with their millions of dollars in ad spending.

Stories sell! You'll hear more about story-based marketing as you read on.

Keep in mind, when I'm giving you examples throughout the book and there's a free meal or discount involved, remember, you should always use restrictions when needed so you don't attract the "coupon cutters" who only come out with a coupon and don't want to spend money. As I go through the LRVO formula in the next section, you'll understand when I use free offers, discounted offers, and no discount at all. There's a time and place for all but I'm not about always discounting. That is a recipe for training your current customers to always look for discounts.

Exposed!
A Startling Fact About (Your Bar/Restaurant)

Here's another newsworthy, curiosity-driven headline. The startling fact could be that you have the best burger and why you have the best burger. It could be a number of things. You just have to be creative to craft your story or message.

How You Can Enjoy a Night Out for Only $xx

Above is a headline that is curiosity-driven and will attract people who are looking for a fun night out. Your marketing message would then explain how they can come to your business and get XYZ for only a certain amount of money.

Why Women in (City) Choose (Your Bar) Over Any Other (Bar/Restaurant)

Remember, your headline is designed to attract the **_BEST_** prospect for your offer or promotion. Not everyone in your area is a perfect fit for what you have to offer.

The headline above calls out women and draws in curiosity. It will get a woman to stop and say, *"I'm a woman, and I want to know why all the women in this city are going to this place over any other!"* That curiosity encourages them to keep reading to find out more about your offer or promotion.

Your marketing message would then reveal the benefits and value of the promotion you are running that is targeted towards women.

Tired Of How Expensive It Is To Enjoy A Night Out? Well, We Want To Give You xx% Off Your Next Tab, So You Can Let Loose, Have Fun, & Enjoy Yourself!

Asking a question in your headline works great because it gets the reader thinking and answering the question. People read this headline and say, *"It is pricey to go out all the time. I am tired of it. This message really resonates with me!"*

The message goes on to hit their emotional desires of letting loose and having fun. They **_start to imagine_** having a good time, and that's what you want!

Video & Radio Advertising Headlines

When you're running video ads on Facebook, Instagram, YouTube, television, etc., the first sentence that comes out is your headline. It's the same with radio. You only have five seconds or so to grab their attention. Almost all of the headlines I just reviewed could be used in video and radio too.

Again, it's all about calling out your prospect and getting their attention with value and benefits or using curiosity-driven headlines that get them wanting to know more!

#2: Valuable Offer

How can you measure the response of your marketing if your potential customer can't take action? You can't. You need to create some way to track your marketing dollars, and the best way to do this is by requiring customers to redeem the offer with a coupon, by showing a text, by mentioning a social media post, by bringing in a postcard, etc.

Your offer could be a percentage off their tab, a buy-one-get-one, no cover for entertainment, a free drink, a VIP invite to a special event you're having for your loyal customers, etc.

Keep in mind, the better and more valuable the offer, the better your conversions will be because more people will take advantage of it. Everyone, including you and me, are _in it_ for ourselves when it comes to doing business with other people. We get hit with tons of marketing from businesses, so all we want to know is, *"What's in it for me?"* When your potential customer receives your marketing message, you want them to say, *"I need to take advantage of this! I can't pass this up!"*

People want VALUE. They need a reason to choose you over anywhere else. I'm not saying you should give everything away, but you need to give a GREAT VALUE to get new customers in the door to "try" you out. Then it's your job to keep them coming back by capturing their contact information and using follow-up marketing systems, which I will cover in Sections Two and Three.

This is important, and I don't want to mislead you: When it comes to attracting new customers, you **MUST** have a _**valuable**_ offer in order to get the best response. When you are targeting existing customers, it _**doesn't**_ have to be a big discount. Your offer could be at a premium price, but your marketing message persuades them on the experience they are going to have when they come in. Most people don't care about price; they care about the experience they will have and how they will benefit from that experience. When it comes to getting NEW customers, however, it does require more effort, which means a value they can't pass up.

#3: Compelling Copy

Compelling copy is words that make you want to read more of an ad. Each sentence makes someone want to read the next.

Here is an example of part of a letter that I send to new residents in my area. Every month I get a mailing list of people who move within three miles of my bars, and I send this letter by mail to get them to start doing business with me before they think about my competition.

Local "Bar or Restaurant" Owner Infuriates His Competition By Giving Away Free Meals In Your Neighborhood

Hey Neighbor,

My name is (Owner Name), and I own "Name Of Bar / Restaurant" in "City". I saw that you had just recently moved into the neighborhood, and I wanted to buy dinner. Why? Because I'm that kind of guy. No, this isn't some kind of buy-one-get-one deal. I'm buying you dinner up to $10.00 off.

You see, I do business different from everybody else. Most business owners are trying to get every penny out of you. Don't you agree? I believe that if I can help people and buy them a meal every once in a while, hopefully they will refer their friends and family. This is my way of trying to prove to you and others that I can live up to my word of providing you one of the best experiences in town.

Are You Like Me?

If you're like me, and just about everyone else, you feel eating at home is boring. You're at work all day, stressed out by your irritating boss, and the last thing you want to do is take twenty-five to thirty minutes of your time to cook your own meal, or even worse, eat another frozen dinner just to save time.

Save Yourself The Hassle & Let Me Buy You Dinner!

This is just the beginning of the letter, but do you see how I capture the reader to keep them interested in reading? You want to create a bond with the reader, and you do this by understanding them and their life. You want to relate to them on an emotional level. When you find a way to stir up their emotions and show them how your offer or promotion could be their solution, it gets them in your doors.

For example, for a bar I brought up how eating at home is boring and how they can get away from that and be entertained. People go to the bar for different reasons: They don't want to sit at home; they want entertainment; they want to talk to people who are like them; they want to get their mind off their nagging significant other with whom they have a bad relationship; they want to make friends, they want to look at an attractive staff; they want to feel like they have a family, a feeling they get from being a regular and knowing everyone at your bar.

Not every bar/restaurant has the same customers, but these are several reasons people go to a bar—and there are a lot more. When you create your marketing message, you need to think about exactly who you are targeting and what emotional triggers you can stir that encourage them to **_WANT_** to take advantage of your offer.

How to Write Your Marketing Messages

When it comes to writing compelling copy, you write to your prospects or customers in the same what that you would talk. Don't write in stiff, formal, elevated language. Write your emails, Facebook posts, direct mail, etc. as if you are having a conversation with them face-to-face.

Your persuasive marketing message is compelling when it communicates that you understand your target market 100% and that you can relate to their wants, desires, and frustrations. In order to get them to take action on your offer or promotion, you then need to <u>persuade</u> them on how they will benefit and **_why your offer or promotion is better than any alternative they have._**

I'm willing to bet you're saying to yourself, *"This sounds hard, different, or strange."* Here's the truth. No, it's not easy to start writing compelling, persuasive copy. It takes time and a little practice. Success doesn't come easy, but once you start doing this, and you see the results of standing out from your competition, it will be fun and exciting for you!

#4: The Urgency/Scarcity

The whole point of marketing is to get customers in your doors and make a return on your marketing investment <u>as soon as possible.</u> In order to do that, you need to create urgency or scarcity to get people to take action right away.

You can create urgency and scarcity in a few ways:

1. Expiration dates: "Offer expires by (date/time)" is most common.
2. "First (specific number of) people in the door," "First (specific number of) people to sign up," etc.

Within your marketing message, focus on making the point that they don't want to miss out, this offer does expire, and that they can't pass it up. People don't want to miss out on good deals or fun times. At the end of your marketing message, your urgency and scarcity message is critical to getting them to take action.

For example, let's say you're giving away $20 gift certificates. You explain why you're doing so and how customers will benefit from the savings, value, and experiences they are going to get. You could then say you're only giving away 10 certificates because you just can't afford to give this deal to everyone. You'd then want to say, *"These will go quick, and if* *you're reading this now, that means they are still available. Once 10 people sign up, this site will be taken down. Enter your information below right now, and we will send you your $20 gift card within 24 hours!"*

This example is something I made up quickly to help you understand how to use urgency and what I like to call "reason why" copy to explain why you're only allowing 10 certificates to be given away.

After you create the urgency, you need a call-to-action. In the example above, that was the call to "sign up now" to get the gift card.

#5: A Call-to-Action

A call-to-action is something that is often missed. Most of your customers are pretty smart people, but there are some who are not. You must tell them exactly what to do to take advantage of your offer.

If you're sending out an email, do they need to show that email or print it and bring it in, so you have a copy of the redemption? If you're sending out a text offer, do they need to show they received it, or do they just come in? If they just come in, you can't track the response of your efforts.

If you're sending out direct mail, an email, or Facebook ads for an offer, do they need to go to a website to input their information in order to get the offer? Do they come in with a coupon? Do they call into your business as a response?

This sounds like common sense, but you'd be surprised! It all boils down to you and how you want to track and manage the response and effectiveness of your marketing. I send out quite a few emails every year in which I write, "PLEASE DO NOT RESPOND TO THIS EMAIL. INSTEAD, EMAIL (NAME) AT (THEIR EMAIL ADDRESS) FOR MORE INFORMATION!"

I highlight that phrase and use bold lettering and ALL caps! I still get a small amount of responses from people saying that they are interested in what I have to offer. Then I have to tell them to re-read the email and who to contact!

To give you a better understanding of how or why I would say this in an email, let me give you an example. I have some promotions that involve pre-selling tickets ahead of time for a dinner or other events. I email my customers to let them know what we are doing, why they need to come, and what they are going to experience. The call-to-action for my offer is to get in contact with my manager to get them signed up and that they should get the payment to us ahead of time.

Bonus Tip for Emails, Direct Mail, Websites, and Facebook Posts

Use testimonials from happy customers within your marketing messages.

You can tell people all day long that you have the best wings, that you have the best staff, that you have the best atmosphere. The only thing they think is that you want their money, and that's why you're telling them those things. They think, *"Prove it! I don't believe it! Why should I believe that?"*

The best way to prove your claim is to use testimonials within your marketing. It's social proof.

A testimonial is a statement from one of your customers about your bar or restaurant. It's a review. How do you get testimonials? Ask your regulars to give you three to five sentences saying why they like your business, how the food is, what the drink specials are like, etc. The goal is to get positive feedback.
You can also gather testimonials from your Facebook or Yelp reviews.

You should be using testimonials in your postcards, sales letters, on your website, video ads, and Facebook ads. People have seen all kinds of scandals, so they are skeptical about what they believe. Using testimonials from others like themselves creates credibility. *It builds your brand in a powerful way.* New customers will believe in you and your business more strongly. Think about when your friend tells you about a great place to eat; you're likely to believe him or her and try it out. ***These testimonials help you create that same effect.***

If you're able to get testimonials from local celebrities, such as radio hosts, TV news anchors, and politicians, you can really boost your credibility. If you don't personally know any, send them a letter and an email saying that you want to buy them lunch, dinner, or whatever item you're trying to promote. You then tell them you are kicking off a new promotion and want to get five or so reviews about their experience, etc. to help the efforts of your campaign.

If they are a big enough authority in your market, even offering a $100 gift card to them would be smart. Chances are, they wouldn't take it, but they would love that type of offer. It would help them understand how important this is to you. Some people really appreciate being able to help others.

Tips When Using Testimonials

1. When using a testimonial, add the customer's first and last name, along with the city they live in. This builds even more credibility. If you don't have a name attached to a testimonial, people will probably think you wrote it.

2. When you quote somebody in your marketing, use italics type.

3. If you can use the person's picture, doing so will boost your credibility even more. It will boost your prospect's ability to believe because they can put a face and a name to the quote.

4. If you are targeting a younger demographic, and you're using video or picture testimonials, make sure your testimonials are from a younger generation. The reverse applies when it comes to older demographics.

5. If you're targeting women, make sure ALL of your testimonials are from women. By strategically planning out testimonials within your marketing based on the target market you are after, you'll boost the response of your ads and get a much higher ROI on your marketing dollars.

Quick Overview

In every ad you need:

1. A powerful headline that attracts the attention of your prime target market for your specific promotion or offer.
2. An irresistible offer, which can be discounts, package offers, or experiences.
3. Compelling copy: Your persuasive message should hit your prospects' emotional triggers and get them to say, "I can't pass this up!"
4. Urgency/scarcity encourages them to take action now and not forget about your amazing offer.
5. A call-to-Action that explains exactly what they need to do in order to get that discount or have the experience you're offering them.

Here's what you don't want your paid advertising to look like:

1. Your logo really big at the top of your marketing: Nobody cares about your logo. People care about what's in it for them. Why should they do business with you over your competition?
2. Only your specials and prices: This is what 99% of the owners who come to me for coaching and consulting do, and it is exactly what I used to do when I was a failing owner. Don't be like everyone else. Be persuasive and build credibility and trust within your marketing. You can't do that by just stating prices.

Conclusion

I know this sounds like hard work—and it is. Nothing is easy at first, but as you work at it, it becomes very easy. It's all about repetition.

The truth is, this is where the money is. Your time is your most valuable asset. To leverage your time and live the life you want, becoming a persuasive marketer is what needs to happen. Having the power to write a few emails or direct mail campaigns and put $10,000 or more in your pocket is a talent every owner wishes they had.

I tell my clients their two main focuses should be spending most of their time overlooking their customers' experiences/getting feedback and focusing on how to become a persuasive marketer. Outsource everything else in your business. Payroll, scheduling, ordering, etc. isn't going to bring you the results you want, and if you use the excuse of not being able to afford to outsource, you'll never be able to until you focus on your two most important jobs.

Let's now move on to section 2!

Section 2:
Loyal Regular Value Optimization

Chapter 5:
Loyal Regular Value Optimization

Imagine yourself on vacation right now. You're in the Bahamas, it's 83 degrees, sunny, your feet are in white sand, and you're watching the turquoise blue water wash up on the shore while sipping your favorite beverage. You're with the person or people you enjoy being around the most.

Sounds relaxing, doesn't it? Let me add to it. You're not thinking of work, and you're not worried about your business. You know your bank account is adding up every hour because your business runs smoothly each and every day thanks to the systems and processes you have in place.

Wouldn't that be a great feeling to have? You would know every day, whether you were on vacation or sitting at home on the couch, that things were running smoothly and that your bank account was growing? Maybe you know that feeling, and you do have systems in place. If so, good for you! If not, it's never too late to start!

Within Section Two, whether your business is running on autopilot or not, I reveal a five-step marketing and promotional system and formula that will bring you more new customers and turn them into loyal customers in the shortest amount of time, with the least amount of risk to your marketing dollars. This formula will give you the ***opportunity to make more money, satisfy more customers, build your brand in the most powerful way, and outsmart your competition.***

Before I go on, I want to make something clear. You should have multiple systems in place within your business: a system for hiring and firing, a system for inventory, a system for ordering, a system for how your employees approach and take care of your customers. I can go on and on, but that's what business is all about: having multiple systems in place that **_run_** **_your business for you, so you can do what you want, when_** **_you want._**

You didn't get into the bar or restaurant business to have the business run you, did you? Of course not! Still, so many owners have broken systems or no systems within their businesses, which causes frustration and burnout, which in turn leads to unhappy lives, lost profits, unhappy customers, and unhappy employees.

When someone buys a franchise, what are they buying? They are buying a system; a proven business model with multiple systems in place that makes them money with the least amount of frustration.

There's a book I highly suggest you read called *The E Myth* by Michael E. Gerber. It teaches how to start implementing and refining systems and processes in your business. It will teach you how to do less work and make more money.

The E Myth was my roadmap to only having to spend two to three hours per week working on both of my bars, so I could focus 40 or more hours a week on Bar Restaurant Success.

My book doesn't teach all of the different systems you need in place, but I do make the point that having multiple systems in place allows you more time off, *so you can focus on growing your business*, and that this is the ultimate key to success and getting everything you want out of your business.

The sole purpose of this book is to give you a marketing and promotional system that takes all the frustration out of marketing and promotions and gives you the easiest and fastest way to grow your business.

Let's start by reviewing the advantages of having a proven marketing and promotional system in place, and then I'll introduce you to Loyal Regular Value Optimization!

1. There is <u>almost</u> no limit to your income besides the capacity of your business! A great sales letter, postcard, or email campaign can bring in $5,000 to $10,000 or more in sales. Once you find one that works, you can produce it as many times as you need to. It's like you're printing your own money.

   Remember what I said about the first sales letter I sent to local businesses? I sent out around 300 letters and brought in over $16,000 in sales, while getting hundreds of brand new customers in my doors. You can systematize those types of promotions year after year or quarter after quarter.

2. You will see an improvement in your staff. They will be very accountable for the success of your new system, and when your bar or restaurant is making more money, that means they are as well. They'll feel good about themselves, and they'll feel important when they understand that they matter to you and your business.

3. You'll control the amount of business you bring in each week. This means you will have the ability to gain new customers each and every week or get existing customers back through the door whenever you want.

4. You can automate your marketing system, so it works for you 24/7. You can easily build instant trust, credibility, and relationships with brand new customers whom you've never met.

Now I'll walk you through the automated marketing and promotional system I use with every single private client of mine, the system that is responsible for the most profitable online marketing campaigns in the industry. I research my competition, I read all the blogs and industry newsletters that I can, and I don't see any case studies or proof of results like the ones you'll hear about from following my LRVO formula.

Loyal Regular Value Optimization (LRVO)

I came up with the name Loyal Regular Value Optimization because the core focus of this system is to attract brand new customers and turn them into loyal customers on autopilot, but it's also to keep existing customers coming back because of your future marketing efforts. Throughout the book, I refer to this system as LRVO to keep things simple and short. I refer to it as a system or a formula because the formula of LRVO is the structure of the New Customer Attraction & Retention marketing system in Section Three.

LRVO is the foundation upon which all strategies in marketing and promotions are built. It is the core to everything I do, and it's critical to all the other lessons, techniques, and strategies in this book and on my website.

If you fail to understand this core formula, then you will fail at applying all of the other concepts I teach. For example, when I talk about Facebook marketing or direct mail marketing, I do that in the context of the LRVO formula.

Take Successful Marketing Models& Apply Them To Your Business!

LRVO is very comparable to the same system that McDonald's® and Best Buy® have used to corner the burger and electronic markets. It's the same system Amazon uses and that made them the e-commerce bully. It's how P90X® became one of the world's top-selling exercise programs, Proactiv® the number-one-selling acne cream, and Sports Illustrated a household name.

If someone told me when I first got into this business that I could apply the same type of marketing and promotional system to the bar and restaurant business as all of these big, multi-million-dollar companies, *I would have thought they were out of their damn mind.*

I'm here to tell you that I've done it myself in my bar/restaurant businesses, with Bar Restaurant Success, and I've done it for hundreds of bar/restaurant owners all around the country. It brought them some amazing results they never thought were possible. You can do it too!

3 Proven Laws of Business Growth

The LRVO formula is genius because it exploits each and every aspect of the three proven laws of business growth.

There are only three ways to grow a business:

1. Increase the number of customers.
2. Increase the average transaction value per customer.
3. Increase the frequency with which customers visit your business.

If the LRVO formula is followed correctly, you'll easily add 25 to 50 new loyal regulars to your business, who spend an average of $200 per month with you. That's about a $60,000 minimum increase in sales.

I'm going to share one case study with you later in the book about a client who did nearly $60,000 in sales and got over 2,000 brand new customers in his doors from just three emails and some Facebook posts—all by following this system. Another client did $30,000 in sales with just three emails and no Facebook posts.

My advice to you is: **Commit this to memory.** Anytime you're planning to run a new promotion to attract new customers or get your existing customers back in the door, follow each of the five steps within this formula. There is little profit in understanding Facebook marketing, for example, or any other marketing strategy in and of itself. There is **enormous** profit in understanding how to apply Facebook advertising to this LRVO formula.

IMPORTANT!!!

Right now I'm going to give you quick overview of the formula in context of targeting brand new customers and turning them into loyal customers, but keep in mind, this formula is also used when targeting existing customers as well, minus step 3 (sometimes). I'll explain more on why "sometimes" as we go. I just want to keep things really simple right now.

In section 4 I'm going to get into a little more detail in order for me to give you the most value. I'll lay out the exact system and marketing strategies I use to attract new customers and turn them into loyal raving fans on autopilot that I use in both of my bars, and in my clients, so you can copy it and implement it into your bar or restaurant business.

Right now I just want you to get the understanding of how this formula works when it comes to attracting and retaining brand new customers and turning them into raving loyal customers.

Here is a flow chart of the LRVO formula. (You can download this in the members' area of the book at www.BrsBookMember.com)

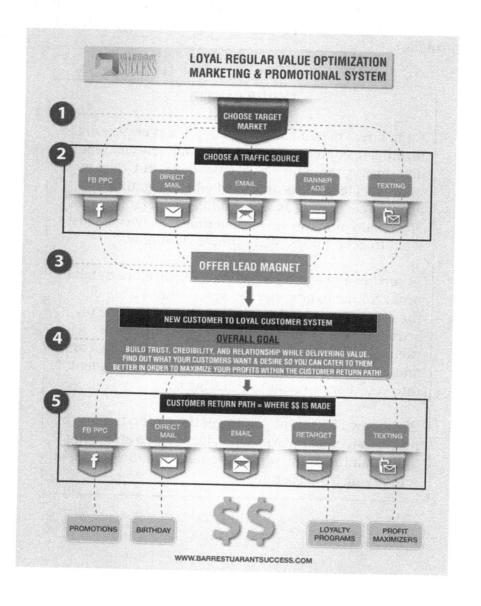

Step 1: Target Market

#1: Who Do You REALLY, REALLY Want to Attract?

Step 1 involves determining who your target market is. Who do you want to attract into your bar or restaurant for your specific offer or promotion? Think back to Captain John Rade in Section One. Don't think like a fisherman; think like a fish. The LRVO formula is all about knowing exactly who you're trying to catch and what kind of bait (offer/promotion) you need to use to reel them in.

With that said, if you want to add another 25 to 50 loyal customers to your business—the types of customers who spend the most money with you—what do they look like? What are their ages and their gender? How much money do they make? Where do they live? These are the questions you need to ask yourself.

In most cases your perfect customer is also your competitors' customer. These customers are people who like to go out to eat and drink, have disposable income, and probably live close to your business. You can't walk into your competitor's bar or restaurant and start giving out drink tickets or coupons promoting your business. That's just not ethical. There is a legal and ethical way to do this, which I'll cover, but before I get into that, I want to make something clear.

When you're creating a new promotion, your market could change. For example, a late-night party promo with a DJ and a new lunch menu have two different types of customers. Keep that in mind with every promotion you do *__because not every promotion is right for everyone. You need to target the people who are more likely to take advantage of what you have to offer.__* I'll give some different examples in the big-money promotions section of the book.

Step 2: Choosing The Best Traffic Source That Will Give You The Best ROI!

Think about the most cost-effective and direct way you can get your offer ___ONLY___ in front of customers who like to go out to drink and eat, have disposable income, and live close enough that they are willing to drive to your bar or restaurant.

Write this down:

> *Marketing is all about excluding everyone who you don't want to do business with or excluding everyone who doesn't want what you have to offer, and **ONLY** targeting the people who do **WANT** what you have to offer. Can you imagine the results of your marketing if you could **ONLY** market to people that **WANT** to do business with you??*

You're probably thinking to yourself, *"Is it really possible to do that?"* YES! Today, privacy is dead. You can buy direct mail lists based on age, gender, demographics, household income, etc.

What's 10 times more powerful and a hell of a lot cheaper? Using "digital marketing." In Section Three, I cover my favorite traffic sources, but in order for you to get the best understanding of how LRVO works, I will give you an example as we walk through each of the five steps here.

Don't let the term "digital marketing" scare you if you're not a tech/Internet user. Soon you'll be in love with it, and you'll start applying it immediately because you'll know how to have someone else within your business do all this for you.

Most Profitable Digital Marketing Strategy

The most profitable way of getting new customers in your doors right now is to use Facebook ads, where you target market to people based on their interests, their incomes, where they live, etc.

It gets even better!

You might be familiar with the Facebook Ads Manager, but what about Power Editor? This is the Facebook advertising platform on steroids and it's revolutionized the way bar and restaurant owners market their businesses. It's saving owners well over $10,000 to $20,000 a year on advertising dollars when using the LRVO formula.

In the Power Editor you can target people in your area with ads, based on gender, where they live, etc., but also by their purchasing behavior using their credit and debit cards. This means that if you want to ***target people buying beer, wine, liquor, or food at other bars and restaurants, you can TARGET ONLY these people with your offers!***

If you want to target males between the ages of 21 and 35, who live within a three-mile radius of your bar, who drink craft beer, and who like football, you can target only those people and put your specific offer out to them.

This is totally revolutionary for bar and restaurant owners, but here's another key component: You ***ONLY*** pay when people click on your ads and offers. This means that you can still brand your business with no cost to you if people don't click. They will see your offers, they will see your brand, but if they don't click, you don't pay!

This is like going to your newspaper or radio ad rep and saying, *"Here's $500. I want to run this ad, but I only want it to be seen or heard by people who are buying beer, wine, liquor, or* *meals at other bars and restaurants!"* Imagine the ROI on your marketing dollars!

Here's a screenshot of one of my client's campaigns, which we just ran to promote their lead magnet. You can see the ad set name on the left. We targeted drinkers and people who "Liked" other bar and restaurant owners' Facebook pages, our two most profitable target markets.

This shows we reached about 21,000 people; we had about 70,000 impressions, meaning our ad were shown to our perfect target market; and we had about 3,700 clicks to our website, where the average cost was $0.20 to $0.08 per click.

Where else can you get guaranteed results hitting your target market, drive them to your offer for $0.20 to $0.08, and exclude just about everyone else in your area who doesn't have an interest in what you have to offer?

On the next page is a screenshot that shows the targeting options inside Power Editor. The interest means people who "Liked" bar and restaurant pages in our area, and the behavior is their ***purchase behavior*** on their credit and debit cards!

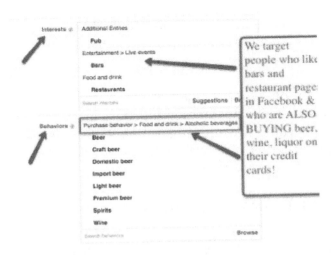

Here's another screenshot of the same campaign that shows the video views. This was a video ad that we ran to our target market. It was only $0.02 cents per view. This is like running commercials on TV—for only two pennies per view to your perfect audience!

They spent less than $500 for all of this, and it was a 30-day campaign!

Here's what's important for you to know: I oversee about $15,000 to $20,000 a month in Facebook ads for my clients and myself. I've run hundreds of split tests on ads and marketing campaigns. Facebook is by far the most profitable **<u>PAID</u>** platform to use when trying to get BRAND NEW customers through your doors.

That doesn't mean simply posting on Facebook, but *PAYING* for traffic. Facebook doesn't give businesses exposure on Facebook anymore because it wants you to PAY, but the price is so cheap and the targeting is so precise that *you'd be out of your mind not to pay for Facebook traffic.*

Step 3: Offer Lead Magnet

How To Attract All The New Customers You Need & Become Unbeatable In Your Market

Let's back up before we move forward, because I know this can be a little confusing. I have you covered! The LRVO formula is all about doubling your loyal customer base, which means you have to effectively get brand new customers in the door.

Step 1 is all about figuring out **WHO** you are going to target for your offer or promotion. Step 2 is knowing which traffic source, what media, is **<u>best</u>** to target the WHO, the new customers you're after. Step 3 is the offer, **_the persuasive message that gets your customer to take some type of action._**

(Refer back to page 49 if needed to see the flowchart)

As I've said before, one of the biggest complaints I hear from owners is that their marketing efforts don't get any new customers in the doors. *They feel marketing is a waste of money.* Ninety percent of the time, this is **because they don't have an offer within their marketing.**

Their advertising just states the promotion, prices, their logo, their business information, and an image for the promotion, but there's no offer that can be redeemed or tracked. If they do have an offer, it's not strong enough to get a new customer to walk into their doors, or the message tied to the offer isn't persuasive— it doesn't help the customer understand how they will benefit.

This Is Important So Highlight This!!

*Any time you market your business to get a **brand new** customer in the door <u>you better have a valuable offer. An offer that out-beats your competition's offer...if you want to get the most amount of new customers in the door!</u>*

How much is a new customer worth to you if they come in once a week, and you profit $20 from each visit? If you multiply that customer by 52 weeks, you profit $1,040 a year. *How much are you willing to spend to get* a $1,040-per-year customer? You could pay up to $1,040 and break even, but that would be insane!

How Much Is A New LOYAL Customer Worth To You?

How much is a customer who comes in four to five times per week worth to you? Let's say, on the low side, they spend $100 per week. That's $5,200 a year. Would you pay $500, $1,000, even $2,000 to get back $5,200 in sales? *Of course you would! You'd do that as many times as you could!*

Let's say a new family of four comes into your restaurant once a month and spends $100. That's $1,200 a year. What would you spend to get that group for three, four, or five years?

"He who can spend the most money to acquire a brand new customer, wins." Jeff Bezos, the founder and CEO of Amazon, once said something that I believe to be a warning to his competitors: ***"Your margin is my opportunity."***

Think Like This And You Become Unbeatable!

The lesson I've learned is that once you understand LRVO (Loyal Regular Value Optimization), <u>you *become unstoppable.*</u> Amazon sells on the thinnest margins, knowing that ***acquiring*** new customers, selling them more, and selling to them more frequently is ***<u>how you become unstoppable</u>***, the three laws of business growth.

You really need to understand how to measure what traffic is worth to you, how much a brand new customer is worth to you, but also how to extract maximum and immediate value from that traffic.

The first goal of the LRVO formula, no matter which traffic source you use, is to drive new "leads" into the LRVO marketing and promotional system. That begins with an irresistible offer or what I also call a "lead magnet".

Powerful Lead Magnets = 3 Times More NEW Customers!

Remember how I said that there are only three ways to increase your business: Get more new customers, get customers to spend more, and get customers to come back more often? ***<u>The lead magnet is designed to get more new, paying customers.</u>***

The lead magnet is an irresistible offer that ***provides value and benefits*** to your new prospect, but in order to get the lead magnet, they must give you their contact information in

56

exchange for your offer. **You want their information, so you can continue to market to them and bring them back in more often to spend more money.**

This lead magnet can be offered in-house at your business or online through a lead-capture website. Here's an example of a lead capture site. It doesn't have to be really fancy; it just needs to state your valuable offer and have a way to capture visitors' information.

If you're using a lead-capture website, you need to have some type of CRM software, like MailChimp, Constant Contact®, Infusionsoft®, etc., that you can integrate into the site so that the visitor's information is stored. Then the software will send automated follow-up emails, direct mail, or texts to deliver your offer.

If you hate technology, don't let that hold you back. In Section Four, I cover more detail on how to streamline this process, what steps to take first, and how to outsource it all.

Now the question is: What should you offer as a lead magnet that will get a brand new customer to not even think twice about handing over their personal contact information in order to get your offer? *The most common way to make this offer irresistible is to give it away at a cost and, in some cases, at a loss to you.*

Your Goal Isn't To Make Money From Your Lead Magnet...Here's Why

With LRVO at this stage, you are **NOT** trying to make a living from your lead magnet. You are trying to acquire new customers because there is **NOTHING** more valuable ___than a list of customers who gladly gave you their information because those people are 300% more likely to respond to your future offers than anyone else.___

Once you understand the rest of the Loyal Regular Value Optimization formula, you will understand how the lead magnet **is the *single most powerful addition you can make to your business***, even though you make *NO direct profit.*

A great example of this is Columbia House® records.

Columbia House took over the music market by making a crazy, irresistible offer that outdid the competition: 13 tapes for $1. They did this because *they understand that **acquiring a**

list of customers is the most powerful asset they will ever have. Now they can continue to market to them with higher-priced products that they are more likely to buy than anyone else.

This is a truth in the bar and restaurant business: The people who gladly hand over their information to you and spend money with you are more likely to respond to your offers and promotions than anyone else. They are the most profitable people on the planet to market to!

One of my clients, Matt Woelfel, who owns a Ground Round Grill & Bar in Waconia, MN, is one of the many clients who's seen a massive impact on his business because of applying a lead magnet offer.

"Nick's done for you marketing & promotional services has far exceeded my expectations. In the first 7 days his automated systems have attracted 846 customers to take action on our first offer online, and within the first 2 weeks we've seen 518 customers use these offers, in which they brought 2 to 3 others with them on their visit. After the first 2 weeks of launching Nick's marketing system, I have seen over $6,000 in sales brought in directly from using the system, while only spending $400 on marketing!" —Matt Woelfel

Now that you know what a new loyal customer might be worth to you, what kind of lead magnet could you offer to acquire a new customer? How much are you willing to spend over your competition to acquire a new customer?

Remember, he who spends more to get a new customer wins! And when you have LRVO in place, you'll be able to extract maximum value as you'll soon learn how to do!

Is this 50% off, good up to $20 off offer better and more
valuable than what your competition is doing? If so, **you're
going to attract way more new customers than your
competition.** If you follow the Facebook marketing strategy I
covered in video two, **you'll easily get your competitions'
customers taking advantage of that offer and walking in
your doors.**

The Strategy Here Is Simple...

The lead magnet strategy is to convert new prospects into paying customers, even at the expense of your profit margin, with the understanding that acquiring a paying customer delivers massive profits through follow-up, "relationship"-based marketing. Again, don't think first-time sale; think lifetime value. *This is where the money is, and now I'm going to reveal how to crank up that lifetime value exponentially!*

Step 4: New Customer to Loyal Customer

The Vital Process To Turn Your Leads Into Loyal, Raving Fans

Let's quickly recap what we've gone over about the LRVO formula. So far you've determined your target market. You've chosen the most reliable and cost-effective traffic source to reach your target market—Facebook target marketing through Power Editor should be number one on your list. You've chosen an irresistible lead magnet, an offer that is more valuable than what your competition is doing, to acquire more new customers at a break-even standpoint.

At this point into the formula, it's **VITAL** that you build trust, credibility, and relationships with the people who are handing over their information to you for your lead magnet. Why? People do business with people whom they like and trust! This is all done through what I call my "new customer to loyal customer automated marketing system."

How To Deliver The Lead Magnet So You Get The Best Results Possible

Once you've captured the customer's information for your lead magnet, you must deliver that offer to them. In the past I always used direct mail as the delivery process, but today we deliver by email because we would sometimes hear that the customer didn't receive their offer in the mail, which sometimes caused issues. Sending the lead magnet offer by email allows us to see whether or not they opened the email, so if anyone ever complains that they didn't receive it, we can quickly find out if they have or have not.

This doesn't mean you can't use direct mail to deliver your offer, and it doesn't mean you can't use an automated text message either. I suggest email to save on the cost of print, postage, and the labor of sending direct mail when you're getting started. As you build your list, there are other promotions you can run to get customers' direct mail addresses.

REMEMBER! You know your target market. If you have an older demographic, then mail would be the better option. If you have a younger demographic, then email could be your better option. This is something you have to decide on.

How To Instantly Create Trust & Credibility

My goal with the delivery of the lead magnet is to get customers to feel like they know me on a personal level, even if they've never met me in person. It's to get them to like me and trust me, as well as to provide them with value and let them know I will be sending them more valuable offers because I value their business.

The other goal is to stand out like no other bar or restaurant owner has ever stood out and to make the customer say, *"Wow, I really like this guy. I want to continue to do business with him! Not only is he generous, but he cares about his customers."*

"Damaging Admission"
The Secret to Instant Trust

Here's a valuable golden nugget for you. When I deliver the lead magnet offer, whether it's by email or mail, I tell customers, *"It's nearly impossible to run a 100% perfect business when you're dealing with cooks, servers, bartenders, etc. There might be a time when you come in, and your meal isn't perfect, or the service might be slow. It's very rare, BUT if you ever have a bad experience, I want to know about it. I want to make it right for you because if I don't know about these issues, I can't fix them within my business."*

This is something I learned called "damaging admission." You talk about something that may not be so perfect about your business, and you're upfront with the customer. Marketing experts use this is to build credibility, to build trust, because the truth is, there's always going to be a time that a new customer walks in and something isn't 100% perfect.

> When you can stand out in your new customer's mind and they understand you care about them, their experience, and you're providing them with an offer that out-beats any of your competitors, ***it's a game changer***.

When you deliver your lead magnet offer and use damaging admission to get personal with them, you're taking the first step to turn them into a loyal regular, making you unbeatable in your market. Doesn't this sound like an easier, more profitable, and smarter way of turning new customers into loyal regulars?

How To Set Yourself Up For Massive Paydays With Very Little Effort & Make Your Customers Love You!

I want you to close your eyes right now and visually picture what we've done so far. We've used Facebook to target new customers within your area who are buying beer, wine, liquor, or food at other bars and restaurants on their credit and debit cards. These are the most targeted, highest-value prospects you can target in the world.

They've seen your ad, and they've clicked on it. You pay practically nothing for this to happen. You take them to your lead-capture website, and they fill in their contact information, so they can receive your offer that beats out all the other competitors in your area.

Please note: Facebook _**isn't**_ the only media channel you can use. I used Facebook as an example here because it's the fastest, most targeted, and most profitable way to get new customers into your doors.

Customers receive your "cheers letter / message" and valuable lead magnet, personalized to them, and you stand out unlike any other owner. You instantly build trust and credibility with them. They say to themselves, _"I like this person. I want to do business with him or her. He or she is honest and delivering great value to me!"_

The end goal is to turn this new customer into a loyal customer, a customer who spends a minimum of $100 or more with you each and every month, or better yet, each and every week.

The Most Profitable
Follow-Up Strategy EVER!

In order to turn your new customer into a loyal customer, you **_MUST_** provide them with a great experience when they come in with your lead-magnet offer, **_BUT_** you also need to continue to deliver specials and promotions that they **WANT** and that deliver value and benefits to them. If you follow up with them with offers and promotions that they **_WANT_**, they'll want to come back more often. You can easily do this with a short survey and automate this process 100%.

Here's how I set up my automated marketing system. Three days after the new customer signs up in-house or online for the lead magnet, we have an automated email that asks them to fill out a very short survey.

Now you might be thinking surveys are a pain in the ass and that people don't like filling them out. This is true to a certain extent, but we do it to benefit them, and they understand this before they even see the short survey! We provide them with great value, and we are standing out like no owner ever has to them. They like and trust us.

They get an email three days later, expressing that we want to know what kinds of specials and promotions they like, so we can cater to their needs. To be successful, it's not about what I want, **but _what my customers want_.** Make this email about them, **not you.**

We see at least 30% to 40% response from this—sometimes more—and it's **_EXTREMELY_** valuable information.

The other VERY VERY important question I ask within the survey is, *"Why do you choose one bar or restaurant over the other?"* Seven out of ten owners would think that price is the answer, but it's not. It's service, atmosphere, and cleanliness.

You might be thinking, *"Nick, what's the big secret? This isn't a secret!"* You're right. Surveys are no secret to this industry, but it's all about how you use them.

Let Them Tell You What They Want & Deliver On It

Once we collect a few hundred automated surveys, which can be within two weeks, we have enough data to know what our market really wants and what kinds of promotions they like. Now we know exactly how to grow our business!

I do include within my survey, *"Please don't put penny beers and free food because we do have insurance, rent, and employees to pay. Please provide us with realistic responses, and we will do our best to cater to your needs!"* This weeds out the non-serious, unrealistic, cheap people.

When I had opened up my second bar, Rural On Tap, we saw a huge response to trivia night. I've always hated trivia nights, but ***it's not about me; it's about them.*** The first weekly promotion we ran was trivia night, and it's our most successful weeknight.

If I didn't have this data, if I didn't ask my customers what they wanted, I could be sitting with an empty bar on Tuesday nights because I thought more about myself than what my customers wanted.

This survey is very, very important because it sets you up for Step 5 of the LRVO formula, which is all about offering profit maximizers, big-money promotions, to increase the average check value, which is the second law of business growth. And Step 5 is all about getting customers to come back more often, which is the third law of business growth.

Step 5: Customer Return Path

The Easiest Way To Add $50,000 Or More In Sales To Your Business In 12 Months Or Less, With Almost Zero Risk To Your Marketing Dollars

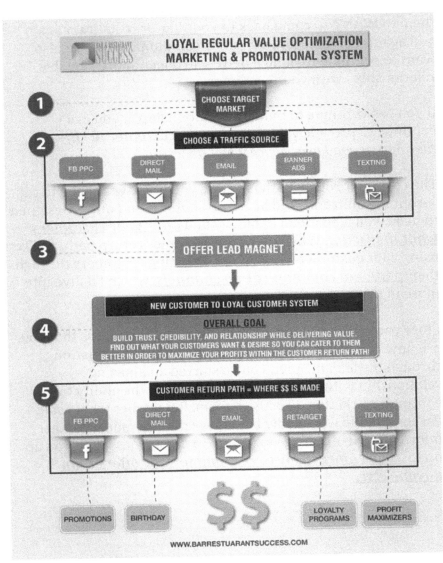

We are now at Step 5 of the LRVO formula, and **this is where the real money is created in this business.** This is also where most owners struggle, or it's something they don't do at all. If you fall into this category, it's **_NOT_** your fault!

The purpose of the customer return path is to have frequent, strategic communication with your customer list that gets them to **WANT** to come back to your bar or restaurant again and again. Don't forget within this communication you also want to continue to build a better, stronger, more valuable relationships with your customers!

If you can continue to build the relationship, if you can continue to provide value, *you have a customer for life—if they have a good experience when they visit.*

The customer return path is where you offer what I like to call "profit maximizers," which are promotions and offers designed to make you a boatload of money and **_offer your customers what they want_**. When using the customer return path, you're using your customer list. You're contacting customers through their **_personal communication channels_**, which I'll dive into more in the next section.

Close your eyes, and imagine the point in the process that you are now. You've received customers' contact information through the lead magnet, you've started an amazing relationship with them, and NOW you have the ability to continue marketing directly to them. Remember what I said earlier: People who gladly hand over their personal contact information in exchange for offers to do business with you are up to **_300% more likely to respond to your offers than anyone else._**

Exactly Why You Want To Focus On List Building EVERY Day You're In Business!

Focusing your marketing efforts on list-building/lead generation 365 days a year is critical to your success. The more people whose information you capture for offers from YOUR business, ***the more money you will make***, as long as you maintain good relationships with them. That's what the customer return path is all about; it's a numbers game.

If you have 1,000 people on your list, and you get a 5% response rate from an email, that's 50 people responding to your marketing. ***If you have 2,000 with the same response rate, it DOUBLES to 100!***

> Marketing is all a numbers game based on response rate. If you're average response rate to EXISTING customers is 5% for your offers, the more people you have to market to the more money you're going to make. I'm not just saying this. It's fact. It's mathematical equation that can't lie!

I've dedicated the next chapter to all of the media channels and strategies you should be using in the customer return path and how to use them to stay in consistent communication with your customers.

I want to leave you with an understanding of the numbers that are a result of applying the LRVO formula to your exact business model and what it will do for you. Then we will get into marketing strategies, big-money promotions, and how to take the first steps to applying this formula to your business, even if you dislike marketing, have no desire for learning technology, or can't spare even five minutes a day to implement this.

Let's Run Some Simple Numbers!

The LRVO formula is about building an unstoppable bar/restaurant business by increasing the value of your customers. Let's run some made-up, simple numbers, so you see how this entire formula brings you a minimum of $50,000 in additional sales within the next 12 months.

Let's say that within three months you build a customer list of 1,000 people who have signed up to get your lead magnet. This isn't hard to do by any means; I've done it for plenty of clients within seven days. I'll go through a case study in a bit.

Over the course of 12 months, after they've gone through the new-customer-to-loyal-customer marketing funnel and you've built up trust and credibility with them, let's just say 5% of the 1,000 customers become loyal regulars.

That's 50 new, loyal regulars.

How much do your loyal regulars spend with you each week?

I'm going to use a bar owner as an example here, but if you're a restaurant owner, a carry-out pizza operation, or anything else, you can scale these numbers to fit your business.

<u>**On the low side**</u> for a bar owner, let's say a loyal customer spends $200 per month with you, $50 per week. If you multiply 50 new, loyal customers at $200 per month, **that's an extra $10,000 in sales per month or another $120,000 per year from a list of 1,000 people.** If you only converted 2.5% of the 1,000 into loyal customers, 25 new loyal regulars, that's $60,000 per year in extra sales.

You know what your loyal regulars spend, and if you're a bar owner, I'm sure it's at least $100 or more per week. When you can follow the LRVO formula and target the right people with the right offers, using persuasive marketing messages and continuing to use your customer list on a consistent basis, it's not hard to add 25 to 50 new, loyal regulars to your business over the course of 12 months, whether you own a bar, a restaurant, a taco stand, or a pizza operation!

Conclusion

Here's the truth about the business we are in and how to make as much money as possible, and I don't care what anyone else says in our industry: **LIST-BUILDING/LEAD GENERATION** is **_the most important and profitable job you have_**, besides *making sure your customers have great experiences when they do business with you.*

Your customer list is the most valuable asset you will ever own. It will allow you to increase sales anytime you want. However, having a list isn't the only thing you need. It's the first step, the foundation.

What will transform your business and your lifestyle? A powerful follow-up marketing system that builds relationships with your new customers and delivers <u>value</u> and <u>benefits. This is what we do in Step 4 of the LRVO formula.</u>

Step 4, the new-customer-to-loyal-customer system, is the secret ingredient to being more successful than you already are and **_making your life easier and more profitable._**

Knowing how to use your list, how to communicate with your list, and how to tell and show your list how you can benefit them will explode your business. **_It's all about the marketing and knowing what it is you're really selling._**

As I said before, service, food, staff, and everything else is important, but if you don't have a *steady stream of new customers coming in* and a way to turn them into raving fans of you and your business, you'll be working way too hard for too little. **_You'll never get 100% of the profits you could be making._**

Now that we've covered the LRVO overview, the next chapter Mike Ganino is going to tell you exactly how to give your new and existing customers the ultimate experience.

Chapter 6:
Creating a Culture of Great Service
Mike Ganino

Why Great Service Matters

If you are following the program from Nick, your bar or restaurant is likely going to be really busy soon. The marketing, social media, and outreach efforts are effective and speedy ways to build and expand your customer base. Maybe your ads and messaging focus on having a great night out, the perfect game experience, or a meal worth raving about. You've made a promise to your customers, so how do you ensure you keep your promise once they pull into your parking lot and enter your venue?

Culture. You have to build a customer service culture within your bar or restaurant. For your team to consistently deliver the kind of experience that makes people come back, it has to just be the way things work. It has to be built into the foundation of the way your team operates. It isn't enough to have just have steps of service, employee handbooks, and reminders scribbled near the employee schedule.

While growing Protein Bar from just one location where my business partner and I worked each day to a brand with locations in multiple states, I knew we needed to create an environment where great service was just part of what we did each day. As we went from one location to four in just four months, customer service and word-of-mouth recommendations were our goal. I knew we couldn't get there simply by smart hiring alone, so we started to develop simple "recipes" that could be replicated at each location to build the kinds of teams that naturally looked for ways to make people happy, solve customer concerns, and stay focused on helping us build our brand.

Don't get me wrong: The marketing, press, and social media all help to make people pay attention to you, but if they come in and have a bad experience, you've just wasted that opportunity, the money spent on ads, and your time putting it together. Service matters, and the best way to ensure it happens is to create a culture of great service.

Creating a Culture of Great Service

When I say "culture," what comes to mind? "Mission statements" and "core values buried deep in the employee handbook" are the most common answers I get when I lead workshops and keynote speeches. Those things matter and certainly contribute to your culture by helping you and your team get clear on how things should be, but culture is a totally separate thing. Culture is the actual pulse in the room or, in this case, your bar or restaurant. Culture changes each day, each shift, and between each team member. It's the temperature and climate of things, which dictates what happens, what doesn't happen, and the way it all goes down.

When I speak at conferences and company meetings, lead workshops on leadership and service design, or consult with bars and restaurants on improving customer service, I always follow a simple (not always easy!) recipe that allows us lots of room to customize their experience for their desired outcome.

You can borrow some of the tips below to try it on for yourself, and if you need a deeper dive session, I'm here for you.

Recipe for a Culture of Great Service

Set a clear and compelling vision for great customer experiences.

If I asked you to go on a trip with me, what would you want to know first? Probably where we were going, right? The biggest mistake I see in so many businesses is a lack of clarity about what the big goal is: *Where are we going?*

I worked with a regional, multi-unit coffee brand that needed help delivering the right kind of customer experience. They were stuck in that "hipster-coffee-aren't-you-lucky-to-have-coffee-at-our-shop" kind of feel that happens sometimes in craft businesses with a hip and trendy vibe. They wanted to be the place known for great service, quality craft coffee, and informative staff. Their service philosophy up to this point was, "Give quality experience and a world-class cup of coffee." It sounds nice, but what is a "quality experience"?

Their philosophy needed more definition, so we wrote a clear vision of what it looked like when a quality experience was happening—not all the steps to deliver it, but how the customer felt.

A good vision will define what success looks like. Give your team room to create that experience; focus on the impact, not that rules/steps; and help point your team towards something.

To get started with your vision, ask the following questions, and focus on telling a story about the experiences:

- What do we want our customers to tell their friends about their experiences with us?
- What does a great greeting and check-in process look like? When a customer is concerned about something, what do they say afterwards about how it was handled?

- What is it like to be your customer? Describe different guest experiences as if they are happening live: people celebrating events, families with kids, event/game nights, older guests. Use these descriptions to shed light on what it feels like to be a customer in your space. Avoid the urge to use bullet points; simply tell the story.

Do this activity with your staff for a way to supercharge your great service culture crafting.

Teach—often!

Once you are clear about the vision for great service at your establishment, it's time to teach it. It is one thing to have clarity and post a note on the bulletin board; it is another thing to commit to training and teaching your team about what great looks like for your brand.

When you are first getting started, why not have an all-staff training session focused on rolling out this new approach to service excellence? Here is an outline for doing that:

- Kick off the meeting celebrating some recent customer service wins (positive reviews, emails, and other comments).
- Give staff the reasons why it is necessary to make changes now.
- Share the visions for customer service greatness from step 1, or create them together in a workshop format, or have me come in and do it for you.
- Roleplay a few of the scenarios, so everyone can try on this new way of thinking.
- Use a whiteboard or big pieces of paper to identify what needs to change to create those experiences.
- Identify and agree on ways to track and reward progress.

Here are some ways to include more teaching into your regular operations:

- ○ *Interviewing:* Include questions around your vision for great service to ensure your candidates share the same ideas. Ask them how they would handle different service scenarios.
- ○ *Orientation:* Spend a lot of time roleplaying around the service visions you created, share stories about great customer experiences, and have staff identify different ways to create those experiences.
- ○ *Initial training:* Most initial training focuses only on the mechanics of service; upgrade yours by focusing on the experience and not just the steps.

Practice it daily.

Most customer service improvement efforts fall flat because nothing happens outside of an initial rah-rah meeting and notice posted on the board. Bring your service vision and expectations to life by incorporating them into everyday activities.

Here are some ways to get started:

- *Daily pre-shift huddles:* Make service a key part of each day by dedicating about 25% of your meeting each shift to a service topic. Best-in-class brand, The Ritz-Carlton has their leadership team cover the same service topic at every meeting across the globe on the same day. If they can do it, you can do it. Pick a great service book, and cover a chapter each week in your meeting.
- *Make it public:* Post and share customer compliments and complaints in public places for the team to see. Make sure to include these in your pre-shift huddles and get ideas from your team about how to keep up the compliments and suggestions on how to improve on complaints.

- *Rethink your systems:* Asking employees to act like owners but then taking away all of their power to make decisions to do what's right for customers isn't going to inspire a culture of great service.

Reward it.

It is easy to notice when things go wrong, and we get pretty good at giving feedback when we need our team to improve. It is even more important to notice when things are right and give your team positive reinforcement, so they know what to continue doing. Your teams take their cues from you and will put their energy towards what you pay attention to as the leader.

- *Frequent feedback:* Give feedback at the end of each shift with each team member before they leave. I learned a really cool method from Zingerman's in Ann Arbor, Michigan. They teach a method called LBNT, which stands for "liked best/next time". At the end of a shift, ask your service team what they liked best about their performances and what they want to do to be more effective next time. Then share your ideas on the same. Challenge yourself to commit to 30 days, and see how your service improves.
- *Gamify it:* Create some simple games that drive sales and increase customer satisfaction. Here are some I've used to help bar and restaurant clients grow their businesses and take advantage of all the marketing efforts:
  - *Perfect check:* A great guest check is one that includes a drink, appetizer, entrée, and dessert. Keep track of every time a server or bartender creates a "perfect check", and enter them for a weekly drawing. Do a product trade with a local business to make it simple and easy.

o *PR:* PR in this case stands for "personal record".
   Set up a contest where each person is trying to
   beat their own sales record. Keep a running tally,
   and give away weekly or monthly prizes.

Review it.

In the bar and restaurant industry. there's a saying: "If you
expect it, then inspect it." The same goes with creating a
culture of great service; you have to review it frequently. By
reviewing it, you can track whether your efforts are moving
forward, if something you've changed is making an impact, and
stay on top of it. I've seen too many brands suffer from not
keeping their eye on the most important part of the business:
the customer experience. What are some ways you can keep
track of your service?

- *Social media:* Make sure you are paying attention on
  social media. In this day and age, it really is less about
  "marketing" and more about customer experience. Stay
  in touch with what is being said about your brand on
  your social media channels.
- *Table touches:* Most table touches are nothing more than
  a quick check on the meal. The common question is
  usually, "Is everything okay?" Smart managers do more.
  Ask specific questions that can help you get a read and
  improve your service; "How was your drink tonight?"
  or, "Was your steak cooked perfectly for you?"

If you are going to do the work, spend the money, and take the
time to run the marketing efforts that Nick teaches in this book.
Then it is important to spend some time making sure your
service will keep customers coming back. Use my tips from this
chapter to upgrade your systems and create a culture of great
service. Within the Resources page of the Membership page for
this book, you'll have access to my guide and checklist
"Creating a Culture of Great Service," or go to
www.MikeGanino.com/servicetips.

Now I want to take you into Section Three, where I cover the marketing medias I use within the customer return path to get the highest ROI. Then we will dive into some big-money promotions and the exact marketing strategies I use to create $10,000, $30,000, up to $60,000 paydays for my clients and how you can follow along, step-by-step!

After that, in Section Four, we will tie everything together into one system, so you can start taking your bar and restaurant business to the next level!

Section 3:
Big Money Promotions & Profitable Marketing Strategies

Chapter 7:
Customer Return Path Strategies

How To Use The Customer Return Path And Create Big Pay Days With Little Risk To Your Marketing Dollars

This is where things get exciting and if you have skipped right to this chapter and you haven't read any of the previous chapters, this section isn't going to do you any good. Here's why.

The way I wrote this book is to start you off to really understand and remind you what **PROFITABLE** marketing and advertising is all about. I wanted to reveal why over 90% or more, of bar and restaurant owners, see very little, if any results from their marketing, and how to stop the madness of losing money. If I've done my job, then you now know and believe that your marketing today needs to be more persuasive and that just blasting out your specials, prices, and logo isn't going to do you much good in today's crowded, skeptical market.

In section 2, I introduced you to the overview of Loyal Regular Value Optimization. A 5 step, marketing and promotional formula that attracts new customers and turns them into loyal customers on autopilot through personalized follow up marketing messages.

Now, in Section 3, I want to dig into step 5 of the LRVO formula with you (The Customer Return Path) and tell you how to create big pay days in your business and give you the ins and outs of the marketing strategies and medias I use that'll get you the highest ROI on your marketing dollars. Keep in mind, the customer return path is where all the money is to be made and it's how you cut your marketing costs by 50% or more, while getting better results, **with almost zero risk to your marketing dollars.**

Right now I'll start off with the media's I use in the customer return path and how I use them, because if I dive into the big money promotions that use these medias and you're not 100% clear on the overall strategy behind them, you'll be very confused when I go over the big money promotions.

E-Mail Marketing

E-mail is by far one of my favorite ways to communicate with my customers because it's very inexpensive depending on the e-mail service you use, and you're showing up in a place that your customer looks every day, if not, every few days - their e-mail box, which is on their phone and computer.

According to (Forrester 2014) 72% of US adults send or receive personal emails via smart phone at least weekly. You can't pass up on NOT using e-mail with those kind of stats and those numbers were from 2014!

According to the Direct Marketing Association, E-mail marketing yields on average a 4,300% return on investment for small businesses in the US!

Exact Target says for every $1 invested on E-mail marketing the average return on investment is $44.25!

You can't pass up on these returns and e-mail should be your primary use of contact within the customer return path.

Here's my predication and insight. If you think about it, everything we do online requires an e-mail address. If you want Facebook or any social platform, you need an e-mail address. If you want to buy something online, you need an e-mail address. As years go on, soon just about every single person in the world who has internet will have e-mail in order to buy online or communicate online and if you have a big e-mail list, you're going to have an asset that will allow you to print money on demand like I said before.

How To Use E-Mail In The Customer Return Path

I typically send out one e-mail every week. Some may say, *"wow, isn't that going to annoy them?"* Absolutely - **_If you do it the wrong way._** The wrong way is sending e-mails and just telling people about your specials and promotions. Blasting out your prices. By doing this it translates to *"Come spend your money here!"* to your customer. There's zero value to them by doing this.

Your most loyal customers may keep opening those kinds of e-mails which will be 15-20% of your e-mail list, but the other 80% or more will not. The way you need to e-mail your customers is exactly how you'd email your mom or your best friend. You open up a conversation with them. You continue to build relationship with them. You deliver value. And that value doesn't have to be a discount every time. More on how to do that in a second.

Important!

I'm **_NOT_** saying don't ever send an e-mail giving your customers an update about your promotions and offers. It's ok to do, just don't make that the point of **_EVERY_** single e-mail. You need to deliver value; you need to be interesting. If not, why would these people take the time to read your e-mails? Let me give you a few examples.

Let Them Know You're Thinking Of Them

Every winter I will get online and search *"How to save on your heating bill"* and I'll find tons of articles. Keep in mind, my bars at the time I'm writing this are in the Chicagoland area, so it's freezing this time of year.

I'll send out an e-mail and start it off by opening up a conversation about how cold the weather has been, how my gas bill has skyrocketed, and that I found this interesting article on *"x ways to save on your heating bill."* I go on to tell them I thought they'd enjoy it and that I was thinking of them.

Then after I told them my story, after I opened up the conversation as a friend would, I'd let them know what we had going on that weekend or what new promotions we had coming. So I'm still promoting but I'm doing it *"Under The Radar"*, **giving goodwill, and building the relationship**. I'm letting them know - *"I was thinking of you and I thought this could benefit you"*, which this has ___**NOTHING**___ at all to do with my business - until the end where you throw in a quick update about your upcoming promotions.

I want you to think about how your customers would think of you for going out of your way to share some valuable information that can help them save money. I want you to think how they would view you. As a friend? Or as a business owner who's always promoting and asking for their money?

The Secret To Profitable Marketing & Building A Raving Customer Base

When you start being viewed as a "friend" from your marketing efforts, you'll double your loyal customers with ease because they will ___**WANT**___ to open your e-mails and they will have received more value and insight from you **than anyone they've ever done business with.** The more you help others and try to be beneficial, the faster you'll see your loyal customer base grow! Don't always think about profit first, think about how you can deliver value and be helpful to your customers, because when you do, the profits will roll in!

That's why the initial "Cheers Letter" I talked about in section 2 is so critical to starting off your relationship with your new customer or even existing customer. Because it makes you standout from every other owner in your area and you're building instant trust and credibility with them - So important!

Let Them In On Your Life & Business

Another approach you should take in e-mails is opening up about your life. Get personal with them. Get them to feel like they know you on a personal level without them even meeting you face to face.

Here's a few ways to start e-mails in a conversational tone that builds trust, credibility, and relationship.

1. Talk about what you did over the weekend - There's times I will start my e-mail by telling them I hope they had a great weekend and then I'll go into something I did with my wife and kids such as boating, taking a vacation, or whatever it is that we did. I'll let them know what's going on in my life. I never talk about the hard or sad things though because then it sounds like you're just asking for attention and you don't want to put your customers in a deep depression lol. You want to always be exciting and fun! Nobody likes to hear bad news, especially if it doesn't pertain to them.

Quick story. I had a lady I never met, ask me about my trip to Seattle at my bar one night. She said it sounded like I had a great time with my godfather (who I was visiting) and then she brought up how she used to live there. Sparked a great conversation and she said at the end, *"I feel like I know all about*

86

you but you don't know me!" That's the goal! People do business with people they like and trust! Trust me, when you do this, you'll experience this too, at least once a month.

2. Talk about something that happened at your bar or restaurant. Did something funny happen? Anything with the staff? The goal here is to start making them feel like they know your staff, your managers, on a personal level.

3. Ask for input and advice.

Here's a really simple e-mail you can send out.

> Subject line would be - Can I Ask You A Question?
>
> The body copy of the e-mail would be:
>
> *First Name, I just wanted to send you a quick e-mail and ask if there's anything you think that we could be doing better at (Your business). I'm always looking for positive or negative feedback. This way I can focus on delivering the best experience, promotions, and specials that you and all our other loyal customers want. If you don't mind, good or bad, please respond back with any input.*

This e-mail would take you literally 3 minutes to type and send and it will give you so much valuable input and make such an impact in the way your customers view you as a business owner. When you show that **YOU CARE** about **THEM** and **THEIR** experience - *it's a game changer!*

Downfalls To E-mail

1. According to www.ExpandedRamblings.com they say the average person receives 121 e-mails per day. This means is you have a lot of attention to fight for with 120 other people in your customers in box. However, if you're following the LRVO formula, you'll be treated like a friend, a family member, and your e-mail will get opened. Keep in mind, your subject line is the **MOST** important part of e-mail. If draw in curiosity or show them there's something valuable inside, better the chances they will open.

2. The average open rate for restaurants and bars, according to Mail Chimp is 21.52% So if you have an e-mail list of 1,000 people, 215 of them will open but the other 785 won't. 2,000 people will be 430 that open. If you can get 5% of that 430 to take action, there's over 20 customers who might bring in 2-3 people with them for your offer or promotion - keep that in mind with these numbers.

I'll explain in a little bit how you can reach all the people who didn't open your e-mail for pennies on the dollar to get your offer or promotion in front of them! This new strategy is crazy effective, yet so many owners are clueless about it because it's so new and nobody is teaching it within our industry at this time.

Don't let those stats scare you though. E-mail is honestly how myself and my clients are able to create multiple $5,000 to

$10,000 paydays multiple times over the course of a year with zero marketing expenses. I just don't want you thinking all you need to do is e-mail because it's so inexpensive. ***You need to use multiple medias.***

Text Message Marketing

I love text message marketing for a few different reasons. Number one, they say 98.7% of people read their text messages within 20 minutes of getting them. That's a huge conversion number!

If you have a text list of 1,000 people, that's 987 reading your message within 20 minutes. Again, 987 people who have said they **WANT** to do business with you. Remember, when you run lead capture promotions, which we will talk more about in a minute, these customers are giving you access to their personal communication channels in exchange for an offer / value to do business with you. This is powerful as you'll continue to see.

Number two, text message marketing is very inexpensive. Most companies out there charge around .05 per text message which is still cheap. You may even get it down to .03 cents if you're sending 10,000 or more texts per month.

As a bonus to members of Bar Restaurant Success Elite - my group coaching program - you can get text message marketing for under a penny per text, with zero monthly fees. It's a pay as you go service through a reputable company I've joint ventured with. If you're interested in learning more about the group coaching program and getting a text service for less than a penny per text, go to www.EliteGroupCoaching.com and get started with a 7-day trial of the membership for only $1 to test it out. If it's not for you, just cancel.

How To Use Text Message Marketing
In The Customer Return Path

1. Send Offers - The best way to see what kind of return you get is to send out an offer. "Show this text and get x" Maybe it's a discount on a tab, discount on a single item, free cover for a band, etc, etc.

Always make sure you have an expiration date within your text to drive urgency and get them in the door ASAP. In the next chapter I'll talk about how we automate our text offers when I give you a 100% full view into the automated new customer attraction and retention system I use.

2. Reminders / Updates - The other way to use text marketing is to just send reminders about your current specials and promotions or updates to new promotions you're running.

I know this goes against some of what I was saying about *"Don't just focus on promoting prices"* but within a text you only have 160 characters to use. So you have to be straight to the point. You can't use much copy to be persuasive like you can with an email, Facebook post, direct mail, etc. Just make sure all your texts are not updates - mix in offers with updates.

3. Send To Website - I've used a text message many times to notify my customers with a link to a website that offers them some kind of value or I'll send them to Facebook and ask if they'd share our most recent promotion.

Retargeting - The Revolutionary Strategy That Can't Be Ignored!

Let me introduce you to a revolutionary marketing strategy that will make all your promotions more successful and **make your e-mail marketing 80% more effective.** This _CAN'T_ and shouldn't be ignored when using the customer return path. You'll see why.

This strategy is called re-targeting! Let me start off by explaining what retargeting is, how it works, and then I'll dive into how I use it.

Retargeting, also known as re-marketing, is a form of online advertising that can help you keep your brand, your offers, your promotions, in front of anyone who has ever hit your website, for pennies on the dollar.

How this works is your website person places a small piece of code on your website, known as a pixel. It's unnoticeable, nobody can see it. You get this code from Facebook or you can get it from Google and other 3rd party companies out there that offer re-targeting advertising.

Every time someone comes to your site, they are "pixeled", which pretty much means we've planted a tracking link into their brain and we can follow them all over the web. I want you to think of this as the lead capture strategy, without asking for their information. I want you to think of retargeting as another way of building a customer list that you can market to again and again.

Later, when your "pixeled" visitors browse the Web, the pixel will let your retargeting provider (Facebook, Google, etc.) know when to serve them ads, ensuring that ***your ads are served to only to people who have previously visited your site.***

Have you ever gone to a website to buy something, such as Amazon, hotels.com, or any other major retail store that's online, and then didn't buy, but you headed over to read another website and you then see ads to what you were just looking at? This is retargeting!

The way most retailers use re-targeting is to target people who didn't buy what they were looking at with ads of what they were looking at. Make sense? We can do the same thing if we are selling apparel, gift cards, or carryout on our website. If they hit the sales page but don't buy, we can follow them with banner ads for 1 day, 2 weeks, or however long you want until they do buy. But from what I see, most bar and restaurant owners are not "selling" online, so I'll tell you how I personally use it in just a second.

Why Retargeting Is So Effective...

Retargeting is so effective because it focuses your advertising on people who are **_already familiar with your brand and who have recently demonstrated interest in doing business with YOU!_** That's why most marketers who use it see a higher ROI than from most other digital channels and that's why I say this is the wave of the future!

All this might sound confusing and trust me, I was confused when I first learned about this too, but let me give you some examples of how to use this within the LRVO marketing and promotional formula.

Let's go back to the beginning of the marketing funnel where we are driving traffic to our lead capture page to build a list of customers.

But let's say they _don't_ opt in. They get to the page and say _"NO, I'm not handing over my information!"_ We can create ads on Facebook that will follow them all over Facebook to drive them back to your site to finish what they started - Signing up to your lead magnet offer.

Google also has a retargeting platform and the way that works is you create banner ads and when your past visitor is on other websites, your banners will be on that site reminding them of your offer.

Here are a few examples of what I mean.

On the next page are a set of the retargeting ads we have set up that follow people all over the web to remind them to come back to our website for our new monthly promotions.

You'll see I have my ads showing up on *The New York Times*

and *Wall Street Journal.* These ads show up all over the web, meaning you can be in front of your customers 24/7. I didn't pay *The New York Times* to place ads there. Google and other re-targeting providers have a display network of website who will pay these other sites money when Google or whoever charges us for the amount of impressions. How much? I'll show you stats in just a second.

So in a nutshell, retargeting is a way to target ONLY people who have expressed some kind of interest in your business already, which ultimately is going to lead you to a higher ROI on your marketing dollars because you're excluding thousands of people who may not want what you have to offer. You can retarget customers on Facebook, Google, Yahoo, Bing, and millions of other websites. This isn't a strategy that should be ignored and it's super inexpensive.

How To Make Your E-mail Marketing 80 Times More Profitable With Re-Targeting

Now I'm going to tell you the other re-targeting strategy I use that will make your e-mail marketing 80 times more powerful! As I said, re-targeting is all about re-marketing people who've been to your site, who've shown interest in your business.

So the other way I use re-targeting isn't to get them back to opt in for an offer but to promote my new specials and promotions. Why? Because it's so cheap and you're nearly guaranteed to get your promotion in front of their eyes because they are searching the internet. _**That's a fact because the only way you could re-target them is they ever hit your website!**_

You should be e-mailing your customers about your new promotions as we already discussed but let's say your open rate is only 20% for this particular promotion, and you have an email list of 1,000 people. There's 800 people **_NOT_** knowing about your event this week right? So this is where re-targeting your list comes into play and allows you to hit those 800 other people who didn't see your ad.

Here's stats from a re-targeting campaign we did for a craft beer event. You'll see the clicks are not that high. That wasn't the goal. Look at the ad. We give them all the info they need. Our goal was to put the info in front of them.

Campaign	Ad Size	Clicks	Impressions	CTR	Cost
	300x250	5	3004	0.17%	$ 4.35
	336x280	2	1145	0.17%	$ 1.16
Beer Events - Deschutes Event	300x600	0	393	0.00%	$ -
	160x600	0	239	0.00%	$ -
	120x600	0	88	0.00%	$ -
	250x250	0	59	0.00%	$ -
	580x400	0	35	0.00%	$ -

So we got over 5,000 impressions, to people who have been to our website, we ran this for 5 days before the event and paid $5.51 cents!

When you utilize e-mail, texting, re-targeting on the web, and re-targeting with Facebook, where you are ONLY focusing on the most profitable people on the planet to market to - Your customer list - you're almost guaranteed a positive ROI and getting your message read by every single customer for less than $50!

What's Important Here...

What I want you to walk away with right now is understanding the strategies to using retargeting.

1. Re-target people who don't opt in for a lead capture promotion in order to get them back to the page and convert them into a new lead.

2. Re-target everyone who hits your website with banner ads for new promotions and updates for pennies on the dollar. By doing this, you can make sure you hit nearly everyone who doesn't open certain promotional emails.

Facebook Advertising In The Customer Return Path

I could write a whole book on Facebook marketing for bars and restaurants, and who knows, maybe that the next one I'm going write, but I'm going to fill you in on the most profitable ways I use Facebook, which is my favorite PAID method of all.

Let me first start off by telling you what most owners I see doing and why it's wrong and why it's right. If you look at all your competitors on Facebook you'll probably notice that you see post after post of pictures of their food, their specials and prices right?

Which this is good to do, don't get me wrong, but only when you're **NOT** paying to show them. What I see most owners doing is "boosting" that "specials" post for $10-$20 or more. They pay to show their specials and prices to as many people as they can, but then they have no idea if that ad made them money or not. They have no clue if customers walked into their doors from that ad. So how do you know if you're making money or losing money? You don't! And that's a recipe for disaster.

The most profitable way to use Facebook ads is "lead generation", as I said before. I've already gone over this in section 2 so I'm not going to go into full depth but as a quick reminder it's where you run ads for a special offer, but in exchange for them to get that offer, they must give you their personal contact information so you can deliver the offer to them, and most important, be able stay in contact with them through the customer return path.

Now I want to tell you how you use this in the customer return path!! And guess what? What I'm about to reveal is even more cost effective and more lucrative then going after brand new customers with lead generation type of promotions on

Facebook. However, this **_wouldn't even be possible_** without running lead capture promotions _so keep that in mind._

Re-Target By E-mail & Phone Number

Facebook allows you to create custom audiences in your ads account. Two types of those custom audiences is E-mail address and phone number. All you have to do is upload your entire e-mail list or text list to Facebook and that will create a custom audience that you can target with ads.

> You might be thinking, well Nick, you're telling me I should be focusing on building my list 365 days a year, isn't this going to be time consuming to update my custom audiences every day? Not at all, there's actually a way to automate this process where every 6 hours your e-mail list is updated to Facebook for you and I'm going to cover later in the book.

The big take away here is this. When you have a new special or promotion, you can target **_ONLY_** the people on Facebook who is on your e-mail list or text list using these custom audiences. You don't have to target 10,000 random people if you don't want. You can focus on the 1,000 to 2,000 people where you spend a lot less money and get ten times better conversions because you're targeting **_ONLY_** people who like you, trust you, and do business with you!

Or, if you wanted to run a new customer marketing campaign and you didn't want existing customers to see specific ads, you can run these ads and **_EXCLUDE_** everyone who is already on your customer list.

Instagram Marketing In The Customer Return Path

If you're not using Instagram, you should definitely make it a goal of yours to start. It's super easy to use, you'll build a bigger fan base, and it's a great way to promote your food, drink, and entertainment promotions. If you're not familiar with Instagram, it's a social media platform that allows you to post images and videos. If people like what you're posting they can start to follow you and like your images and videos. There's a lot more to it, but again, we are focusing on the customer return path and I don't want to get you off point so I'm going to keep this simple.

Why You're Losing Profits & Customers If You're Not Using Instagram

According to adweek.com Facebook has 1.59 billion users (2015) and Instagram has 400 million, which is the 2nd largest following on social platforms. Twitter comes in at third with 320 million.

According to statista.com 22.9% of the users of Instagram are 18-24, 25.6% are 25-34, 19.4% are 35-44, and the other 16% or so are 45 and older. You know the demographics of your customers so these facts should help you determine if you should be using Instagram or not.

If you didn't know, Facebook bought Instagram back in 2012 for about a billion bucks and because of this, Instagram now interacts with Facebook's ad platform.

With that said, when you run ads to your e-mail list, text list, or anyone who has hit your website, **you can now choose to put those ads on Instagram at the same time you're creating your Facebook ads.** You don't have to use 2 platforms, you don't have to create 2 ads, all you have to do is choose to advertise on Instagram when you're creating Facebook ads. Super simple.

Direct Mail Marketing In
The Customer Return Path

Direct mail can be very rewarding, but it can also be very costly if you do it the wrong way. Remember, right now we are talking about marketing strategies to use within your "customer return path" where you're marketing to people who like you, trust you, and **_want_** to do business with you.

This means the odds of making a profit or at least breaking even on your direct mail efforts are much better than sending out direct mail to a bunch of random people who may have never heard of you. I've heard many horror stories of "direct mail" is a waste of money from hundreds of owners. If you have your own, I'm hoping you at least test a strategy or two I'm going to share with you.

Here's a few stats you should know about direct mail.

1. Being personal is still supremely important in marketing. A staggering 70% of Americans say snail mail is more personal than the Internet, according to the Direct Marketing Association.

2. Not everyone sorts their mail over a waste basket. About 56% of Americans say receiving mail is a real pleasure, according to DMA research.

3. Direct mail is also an effective way to woo new customers. 39% of customers try a business for the first time because of direct mail advertising (DMA)

4. You might be surprised to learn that as many as half of US consumers prefer direct mail over email, according to an Epsilon study.

5. According to a USPS study, over 60% of direct mail recipients were influenced to visit promoted website – with the greatest influence on first-time shoppers.

6. Emails are easily ignored. On the other hand, many people actually open envelopes. 70% to 80% of consumers polled by the DMA in 2014 say they open most of their mail, including what they label "junk."

7. Direct mail compels action. The USPS found that 23% of direct mail recipients visited the sender's store location.

8. The USPS study reveals that direct mail recipients purchased 28% more items and spent 28% more than non-direct mail recipients.

9. Almost 60% of online shoppers enjoy receiving catalogs, according to the USPS. Score one for creative departments everywhere.

10. Take nothing for granted. Just because young people dominate the digital sphere doesn't mean they have no interest in good ol' snail mail. Another study found that a whopping 92% of young shoppers say that they prefer direct mail for making purchasing decisions.

What I've Found To Yield The Highest Returns From Your Direct Mail When Used Within The Customer Return Path

1. Newsletters work great! Send out a monthly newsletter or oversized postcard that tells your customer about all your new specials and promotions. If you want to do this with NO money coming out of your pocket, partner with 4 other local businesses who want more exposure and add their flyer or a spot on your oversized post card that promotes their business. If your mailer costs you $1,000 and it's going to 1,000 people, you tell your 4 partners it's only going to cost them $250 where it would usually cost them $1,000 to do on their own!

   Here's another little bonus tip for you. To add more value to your new direct mail partners, tell them you'll send out a monthly e-mail to your e-mail list that promotes their business and a featured Facebook post on your page. The more exposure you can give them, the better the value, the easier you get people to say yes. We ALL want a good value for what we pay for, right?

2. Rip Cards - These are long 3.5 x 8.5 postcards that have a perforated card at the end that measures 2 by 3.5 inches. These are perfect for sending out offers because you can make the perforated end the offer that they rip off and bring into your bar or restaurant.

   If you've never seen a rip card, contact your local print shops or Google "Rip Cards" online and you'll see what I mean.

3. Invitations - If you are launching a new weekly special or a special event, send out a nice invitation in the mail. These cost a little bit more, but when they show up in the mail like a wedding card, it makes your customer

feel really special. To add to that, nobody throws away mail that looks like invitations. Remember, through your marketing you're always looking to build trust, credibility, and relationship with your customers. This invitation strategy is the perfect way to do that and stand out from the competition.

YouTube Re-Targeting In
The Customer Return Path

YouTube re-targeting can be extremely effective for very little money.

Remember how I talked about Google and their pixel you can place on your website that will allow you to re-market to anyone who has hit your website? Well you can run video ads / commercials to all those people who are watching any kind of video on YouTube.

The way this works is your video ad will pop up before the actual video that they clicked to watch - this is called a "non skippable in-stream" ad because the viewer has no option but to watch it as long as the video is 30 seconds or less. Then there's the "skippable in stream ads" that allows the viewer to stop watching after 5 seconds.

There's other types of ads you can run on YouTube as well like the "in-display" ads. This is where your video ad will be on the side bar of the YouTube page, and these tend to be a little cheaper, but don't get as many clicks.

Here's an image on the next page of stats for some in-stream and display ads that we ran for a promotion.

Ad group type ?	Impr. ?	Views ↓ ?	View rate ?	Avg. CPV ?	Cost ?
	10,505	209	1.99%	$0.12	$25.0 M
In-display	7,671	113	1.47%	$0.05	$5.16
In-stream	684	60	8.77%	$0.31	$18.35
In-stream	35	13	37.14%	$0.04	$0.52
In-display	967	7	0.72%	$0.04	$0.29

We had a total of 209 views which cost us $25. So that comes out to an average of .12 cents per view. Again, this was targeting **ONLY** people who have hit my website for our promotion.

In just a second I'm going to give you an example of what it could cost you to kick off a new promotion using all all these medias within the customer return path vs using traditional media outside of the customer return path.

100 Other Ways To Market Your Bar or Restaurant

There's a hundred or more other ways to market your bar or restaurant using Twitter, Pinterest, Yelp, keyword advertising, and all the other restaurant review sites out there. I'm not going to cover them all because I want to give you what I know works the best for me and my clients. Again this chapter is about marketing strategies and medias to use within the customer return path to get existing customers back in the door.

How To Use The Customer Return Path To Market Your Next, New Promotion For A Fraction Of The Cost Of Using Traditional Media, Outside Of The Customer Return Path!

We just went through all the marketing media's / traffic channels, and strategies I use within the customer return path. A lot of information to take in right? Well let's put all this together to make this super easy to understand in an example of how I work with private clients to pick up a slow night of the week.

Let's say Thursday nights are slow, you want to at least double sales for this night, and you're ready to kick off a brand new menu item or special that they can only get on Thursday nights.

You're persuasive marketing message is going to be a discount to come in and try it out, telling them the experience they are going to have, why they should attend, and why your promotion is a better alternative than anything else they could be doing. ***You're telling them all the ways they will benefit!***

Within the marketing message I'd have an offer. So in each traffic source, I'd make sure I could track and manage my results in some way or another. I'll explain more below.

Remember what I said before in the previous chapter, you're marketing message ***doesn't always have to be a discount***. It could be a premium price where you're focusing on the experience. But here I'm going to use a discount.

Here's how you'd use the customer return path going through the LRVO formula.

#1 Send E-mail

Send out an e-mail to your customer list with a curiosity based e-mail with a subject line saying something like - Did You Hear About This? Then the e-mail would reveal your new promotion with the persuasive marketing message that delivers VALUE!

I'd tell them to either show the e-mail by phone or print it off and bring it in to get "offer" on the promotion.

Cost: Depends on what you pay for your e-mail service but I look at this as a free service because what I use for e-mail marketing also automates my entire LRVO marketing system, which as I said, I'm going to tell you about in the next chapter. However, let's just call it $5 for each e-mail you send.

#2 Send Text Message

I'd suggest sending a text message at least 2 days before announcing the new special and price. Then I'd send out a text the day of to remind them and say if you show this text, you get "offer / discount" on promotion.

Cost: If you have a text list of 1,000 people and your text service is at .05 cents per text and there are two texts you're sending out in the first week of the launch, you're looking at $100.00 in texting.

As I said before, if you're part of the Bar Restaurant Success Elite coaching program, you could get texting at less than a penny per text. So if that was the case or if you're getting that price now, to keep things easy, let's say $20. If you want more info on becoming a member go to www.EliteGroupCoaching.com

#3 Set Up Facebook & Instagram Re-Targeting Ads

If you're used to running Facebook ads to 5,000 or more people, then you probably know it costs at least one hundred bucks or more to hit all those people with your ads for them to at least see them twice.

This is going to be totally different, a fraction of the cost, because now we are marketing only to 1,000 people who like you, trust you, and want to do business with you. I'll tell you what it's going to run you in just a second but let's first talk about how long you should run these ads.

I would start running these ads about 5 days before the promotion and your marketing message is going to be directed towards your customer list! Within my Facebook ad, I would include my persuasive marketing message, but I'd also say *"...because YOU are one of our loyal customers, you'll be getting a text and e-mail with a discount / offer of "x" so be on the lookout for it!"*

Remember, you're **NOT** marketing to the masses. You're marketing, having a conversation, with existing customers or people who have given you their info in exchange to do business with you. ***Your messaging is more personal.***

I'd also include at the very end of the message "—-> *Please Share This Post With Your Friends. We Truly Appreciate Your Support & Can't Wait To See You On Thursday!*" By adding this in at the end, you'll get a huge response in shares and comments because you're ONLY sending this message to those who like you, trust you, and want to do business with you.

Cost: I'd start this off at $50 for the first 5 days if you're retargeting list is 1,000 people. This cost would go for both, Facebook and Instagram since you do all this under Facebook's ad platform.

How to track results with no offer tied to it? The only way to measure results with this type of marketing message is to look at your Facebook stats and see how many people saw it, liked it, shared it, and commented. In order to get the ROI on your marketing dollars, tie this $50 into the total marketing budget vs the sales brought in for the first night of the promotion.

Re-Targeting Banner Ads

I'd set up re-targeting banner ads with Google's Ad display to make sure anyone who hasn't seen my e-mail, at least see's my banner ads. The banner ad would simply state what the promotion is, date and time, and then of courses branded by your business. Very similar to the re-targeting ads I showed you in this chapter.

My goal with re-targeting banner ads is to just stay in front of my customer and remind them about my promotion. However, if people click on banner ads, they need to go somewhere because banner ads are made to be clicked. So I will have all the clicked traffic from the banner ads lead to my website with the flyer for the promotion that has more information.

Cost: As I showed you previously in this chapter, we got over 5,000 impressions for that re-targeting ad for $5.51. So let's just call it $10 which should be plenty to show up in front of your customer list a few times and I would have these run 5 days before the promotion kicks off, all the way to the day of.

Overview & Total Cost

When I kick off a new promotion, I always focus on my customer list first because it's not uncommon to get 5%-10%, or even 20% of your list to take action on your promotion. This may sound crazy to you, and I'm going to show you proof of this in this book, but keep in mind that all of these 1,000 people like you, trust you, & want to do business with you - If you're putting them through the new customer to loyal customer marketing system I told you about in section 2. Marketing in the customer return path is a total game changer for what you spend and the ROI you get back!

I will usually hold off on direct mail with the launch of the promotion because direct mail is a bit more then digital advertising. Let's say $1 per mailer if it's a letter with a first class stamp. If I see my promotion could use a boost after a few weeks, I'll send out a letter with another redemption offer so I can track and manage the effectiveness of my direct mail campaign.

Rough Estimate Of Total Cost Of A 1,000 Customer Return Path Launch Campaign:

E-mail - $5
Texting @ .01 x 2 times = $20
Re-Targeting Facebook & Instagram Ads = $50
Re-targeting Banner Display Ads = $10
Total = $85

Rough Estimate Of Total Launch With Traditional Media Targeting New Customers, Not Using The Customer Return Path Media

Every market is different when it comes to radio, newspapers, billboards, etc., etc. so I'm not going to put any kind of number down. You know what your advertising sales reps charge you and you know what it costs you for social media efforts that you are doing now.

I can almost guarantee, you're well over $500-$1,000 to kick off a new one-week promotion if you're aggressive. You may be reading this and saying *"No, I'd only spend $200 or less!"* And if that's true, how are your results?

Conclusion

Having a customer list of people who like you, trust you, and want to do business with you is going to be the <u>fastest and easiest way to crank up sales and cut your marketing costs in half.</u> The example launch campaign I just gave you is the exact type of launch I do for my own bars and my client's bars and restaurants. ***I highly suggest you follow that step by step.***

At the very least you should see a 5% response, 50 people in this example, come in for your promotion. I don't want to mislead you, but this is also considering the promotion you are running is what the market wants. As I've said before, before I ever run a brand new promotion, I always get feedback from staff and customers to make sure there's a hungry audience.

There's no reason at all you can't start to increase certain week nights or days by 20% or more when you focus on this launch strategy for at least 4 weeks. Then when your sales are up, you can start targeting brand new customers with your promotion if you need to, but what you'll want to do is use a lead capture strategy for this. Maybe it's 50% of certificate for that promotion good up to $20 off or $10 off.

I'm sure you know why you want to use a lead capture strategy but I'll say it again, when targeting NEW customers, your goal should be to get them into your marketing system because where all the money is made is in the customer return path. Break even on the front end to get the contact information you need to create a lead, ***then make all your money for months, even years to come through the customer return path marketing process.***

Quick Story That Will Set You Up For Big Money Promotions

This is a game changer & an eye opener. Before I get into big money promotions, I want to share with you a piece of a newsletter that I have, from one of the greatest marketers / copywriters of all time, the late, great, Gary Halbert, where he talks about having a hamburger stand and his one advantage he'd have over his competition. This story is perfect to set you up for the next chapter and to conclude what I just said about *"this is also considering the promotion you are running is what the market wants."*

Here it is:

As you may or may not know, every once in a while I give a class on copywriting and/or selling by mail. During these classes, one of the questions I like to ask my students is: *"If you and I both owned a hamburger stand and we were in a contest to see who could sell the most hamburgers, what advantages would you most like to have on your side to help you win?"*

The answers vary. Some of the students say they would like to have the advantage of having superior meat from which to make their burgers. Others say they want sesame seed buns. Others mention location. Someone usually wants to be able to offer the lowest prices.

And so on.

Whatever. In any case, after my students are finished telling me what advantages they would most like to have, I usually say to them something like this: *"O.K., I'll give you every single advantage you have asked for. I, myself, only want one advantage and, if you will give it to me, I will (when it comes to selling burgers) whip the pants off all of you!"*

"What advantage do you want?" they ask.

> *"The only advantage I want,"* I reply...
>
> ## *"Is... A Starving Crowd!"*
>
> Think about it. When it comes to marketing, the most profitable habit you can cultivate is the habit of constantly being on the lookout for groups of people (markets) who have demonstrated that they are starving (or, at least hungry) for some particular product or service.

Makes complete sense right? If you ***don't have a starving crowd***, a market, that wants the type of offer, promotion, or entertainment that you're providing, no matter how much you spend, ***you won't get a positive response***. You must have a hungry crowd who's excited for what you're offering them.

In the next chapter we are going to talk about big money promotions and at the start of this chapter, I'm going to give you a simple strategy to find out if you have a starving crowd before you ever run your promotion! ***Meaning I'm going to give you a very simple opportunity to almost NEVER risk a penny of your marketing dollars when launching a brand new promotion!***

Chapter 8:
Big Money Promos

This is going to be an exciting chapter! In 2016, I got an email from Jon Taffer, telling me how he was partnering up with the National Restaurant Association and asked me to be a speaker at the biggest show in the country! The topic he asked me to cover was "30 Powerful Bar Promotions in 45 Minutes!"

I was shocked and honored when I got his email, and then I started thinking, *"30 powerful promotions in 45 minutes? Is that a typo? Did he mean 1 hour and 45 minutes?"* Still, when one of the biggest industry leaders asks you to do something that will benefit the industry, <u>*you don't ask questions; you just do it!*</u>

I based this chapter on that presentation I gave in Chicago. I picked out the biggest moneymakers that just about any bar or restaurant owner can do within the customer return path we just covered.

In one of these promotions I reveal how multiple clients of mine generated $10,000 in sales and up to nearly $60,000 in sales with zero marketing expenses. I also go into detail about how online promotions work and why you can't ignore them.

If you're not a tech savvy person, that's okay. Later in the book, I help you with a step-by-step game plan to get other people, such as local web developers, to do this stuff for you!

Survey to the "A or B" Campaign

If you skipped the "Starving Crowd" story in the last chapter, go back to the bottom of page 111df, and re-read the end of the last chapter. It has everything to do with what I'm about to tell you.

The survey to the A or B campaign isn't your typical promotion; *it's a way to know almost 100% whether the next promotion you run will be successful or unsuccessful.* This is a campaign/strategy that you should use several times throughout the year.

As I stated in Section 2, three days after you get a new customer to hand over their contact information to you, you send them an automated email from the owner, saying that you really care about delivering to your customers' wants and desires and that you are in the business for **THEM**. You want to give them the best experience you possibly can. You then say that in order for you to do that, you need to know what kinds of promotions they like. You ask them to take 10 seconds out of their busy day to fill out a short survey.

Then you look at all of the survey results from when you first launched the LRVO formula within your business and look for a pattern. What is it that your customers want most? After reviewing 500 to 1,000 responses over 30 days, you start to get a pretty good idea for what your customers really want. You get a good idea of what new promotional ideas you can test.

After you have this information, you select two of the most common promotions that people said they wanted and send them an e-mail saying that after looking at "x" responses to our surveys, the top two promotions that people requested were either A or B. Of course, you would explain what A and B were within the email.

Within the email, you put two clickable links for the promotions and ask your email list to pick which promotion they'd like to see you do. Then you wait approximately five days to see the final results of which promotion has the best response. When you look at your email software, you can see exactly how many people picked A or B and know the winner without counting or looking at every response!

Here's a quick example how I've used this myself. Every year we run a Crock-Pot® cook-off where our loyal customers compete for who has the best recipe. We've done soup, chili, and any other type of recipe they can cook in a Crock-Pot.

Last year I sent out an email letting my customers know we were at it again—it's a yearly promotion—and that we couldn't decide on soup or chili. We asked them to click which one they'd want to come in for. Soup pulled about 73% over chili. What did we do? ***We gave our customers what they were hungry for!***

Key Takeaway

I want you to really think about what you're reading. I don't want you to just skim, reading as fast as you can ***because this is one of the most profitable strategies you can implement in your business.***

Right now we are asking people who have personally given us their information in exchange for an offer to do business with us to tell us what kinds of promotions they'd like to see us do ***that we are currently not doing, so we can give them better experiences and hopefully meet their needs.***

Then we are emailing them a second time, about 30 days or so later, after we have enough people in our system, to say, *"Based on our survey results, everyone wants promo A or promo B. Can you click either promo A or B in this email to tell us which you'd rather see us do?"*

The key takeaway is that you're going to get the most qualified and profitable people in your area to tell you which promotion they WANT and are willing to come in for and spend more money with you.

I've even taken this a bit further with certain clients. After we complete the A or B campaign, we ask what specific night works best for them. ***This amounts to the "Starving Crowd" I talked about earlier - telling you what promotion they will come in for and what night is best for them!***

This strategy is how you <u>*almost*</u> eliminate any risk to running your next big-money promotion because ***you take all of the guesswork out of knowing whether people will show!***

Keep in mind, the A or B campaign can be run any time. For example, if September is almost here, and you're stuck between two different football promotions, you could easily send out an email telling your customers that you're stuck between two different promotions. Let them decide for you! This stops you from running the promotion that has the least amount of interest.

The Solution: 3-Step Email Campaign That's Responsible For The Highest-Grossing Online Promotions In Our Industry With Zero Marketing Expenses

This promotion is my favorite and what ultimately saved me years ago from almost losing my first bar. I call this *"The Solution"* because it's what solved my sales problems and hundreds of other owners' sales problems.

What I'm about to reveal is exactly how we generate the highest-grossing email promotions in the industry, and it's so simple! Anyone can do this type of promotion.

Here's what the solution looks like

THE SOLUTION

It starts off with the lead capture promotion, then it goes into the new-customer-to-loyal-customer marketing system that we covered in Section Two with the LRVO overview.

Next, we send out three emails within the customer return path that tell a story to our customers about how we are running a party package giveaway promotion and why we are doing so.

Within these emails we use "The 5 Key Ingredients" that you read about in Section One. Keep that in mind that the results you're about to see *wouldn't be possible without a list of customers who want to do business with us and without persuasive marketing messages that contain these five key ingredients to successful ads.*

The goal of these emails is to get customers to click a link in the email, saying, *"Yes, I want a chance to win this party package offer!"* When they click this link, they're taken to a lead-capture page to get them to sign up to win.

After they sign up to win, they are sent an email right away that tells them they are one of the winners, BUT they need to take one more action. They need to click one more link in this new email that will take them to a form to pick out a date and a

118

time, a type of party, approximately how many people would attend, etc.

Will everyone have a date and time figured out? Will everyone be guaranteed the time and date that they pick? Absolutely not! The point is to segment the sign-ups based on who's very interested versus who signed up but didn't take the second action.

Here's a few images of what The Solution looks like within our system when we set it up for our clients.

Scotland Yard Pub

459		77		0
⌒ 0		⌒ 0		⌒ 32
Scotland 3 Step Sequence	Scotland Party #1	Scotland Party Seq	Scotland Yard Party #2	Scotland Party Booked Seq

> "Nick's 3 step e-mail campaign he gave us brought us between $10,000-$12,000 in additional sales"
> **Terry, Owner Scotland Yard Pub,**
> **Rochester, NY**

Riverview Raw Bar

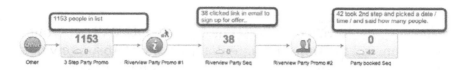

> *"Nick gave us a 3 step e-mail campaign to run that was designed to get smaller groups of people in our doors and after he sent them out for us, it brought us around $13,125 in additional sales over a 5-week time period. We saw around 875 people walk through our doors, just from this!"* **Jason Walker, Owner Riverview Raw Bar & Chill, Charlotte, NC**

Ground Round

I have a 25-minute video in your member's area that explains this in more detail because it's easier to explain through video, but let's look at Ground Round for example.

Here's the link to your membership area
www.BRSBookMember.com

He had an email list of 1,291 people. Remember that in Section Two we spent $400 in Facebook ads on his lead-magnet promotion; 518 of those offers were redeemed with two to three people. He had over 1,000 customers walk through his doors, and he generated over $6,000 in sales from his lead-magnet promotion, which was 50% off, good up to $20 off.

The second promotion that we ran about 45 days later was The Solution. We sent three emails to 1,291 people. By looking at the numbers, you can see a total of 237 people took action. One hundred and fifteen people signed up and didn't take the second action. One hundred and twenty-two booked their parties, taking that second step.

> *"It took us about three months to have all the parties from The Solution campaign. After 27 years being in the restaurant business, I would have never expected anything like this to ever happen. We did a little over $30,000 in sales, we had hundreds of customers walking in our doors, and we didn't pay one penny in advertising to do it!"* —**Matt Woelfel Owner Ground Round; Waconia, MN**

This next one is my best success story yet! But keep in mind that we did use some Facebook ads in addition to emails.

> *"In just 10 days we had 494 people sign up to book parties from just one strategy Nick created for us. Out of those 494 people 265 actually followed through with booking the party and showing up. We are an upscale restaurant, fine dining, so our average party size was about 15 people and they all averaged to spend $15 in cocktails and beer. The end results, give or take $5,000 or so was $59,625 and brought in just about 4,000 customers in which at least half of them were new customers we've never seen."* **Kevin Munz, Cullen's Steak House, Houston, TX**

5 STEPS TO THIS PROMOTION

Step One: Create a party package offer that is more valuable than what your competition is doing. Create a big value that customers can't get anywhere else and that makes them say, *"I can't pass up this deal!"* – but make sure the offer still allows you to make a good profit. Figure out what restrictions you need to tie to the offer and how many people it's good for, and put an upsell package in place to try to boost the average check size.

Step Two: Create a lead-capture page where people will go to sign up to win. All you need on the lead-capture page is a headline saying what the promotion is and what the offer is. To create scarcity, add in that there are only "x" winners.

Step Three: Send three emails to your customer list about the party-booking promotion. Say that you're only giving "x" away, and drive them to the lead-capture page to sign up.

If someone signs up right away, the system won't allow them to receive any more emails asking them to sign up. (Don't worry about the tech details; you don't need to know how that works. All you need to know is how the promotion works. You can have someone who knows about the tech details do this for you!)

Be sure to use the five key ingredients to successful ads within these emails. This is **_VERY_** important to getting the results you want.

Step Four: Create an automated follow-up email after a customer signs up that asks them to take one more action to segment who is serious and who's not. You want to find out what type of party they'd like, how many people they want to bring, and a date and time that work for them.

Step Five: Follow up, and book the party! The contact information from the people who take the second step is sent to you or a manager, so they can call those customers to get their parties booked.

If a customer doesn't take the second step, even after receiving a few reminder emails about taking the second step, you will get an email giving you that person's information, along with a message saying they haven't taken the second step. At that point you have a manager follow up with them to see if they are still interested in getting their party package.

Your ultimate goal is to get as many parties booked as you can because each person who books a party is doing all the marketing for you. They're calling all of their friends and family and bringing them into your business.

You'll have hundreds, if not thousands, of customers walking in your doors, and you know what's going to happen? When you give them great experiences, people are going to start thinking, *"Uncle Bob's birthday is next month. We should have it here!"*

Soon your bar or restaurant will catch a huge buzz as <u>"The Place"</u> to host parties and events.

What Kinds of Results Should You Expect?

I won't guarantee that you're going to make $10,000 in sales from this promotion because I don't know what kind of business you run, I don't know your numbers, etc.

Here's what I can guarantee you: If you have a list of customers who've gone through the LRVO formula, you have a new-customer-to-loyal-customer marketing system in place, and you run The Solution promotion, this will be one of the highest-grossing promotions you've ever done.

Big-Prize Lead-Capture Promotion

This is a promotion that any bar or restaurant can run, and it's a great way to continue building your list while getting your current customer list back in the door for something fun and exciting that benefits them.

The most important part of running this promotion is picking the right "big prize" to win. If you do a big-prize giveaway with a prize that doesn't interest the types of customers you're after—or your current customers—it will be a flop. It's important to pick something that is in line with your brand and business model.

For example, if you own a place that specializes in craft beers, one of your giveaways could be a paid trip to a brewery within 60 miles of your establishment. You take care of gas, the hotel, and entry to the brewery. Much of this expense could be covered by your vendors, so don't brush it off as too expensive for you.

The prize I give away the most is a flat-screen TV because it's a prize that so many people would like to win. You could do vacation giveaways, $500 gift cards, etc. We've even done a diamond giveaway around Valentine's Day and joint ventured with a jeweler to give us diamond ear rings to give away. There's really no limit.

What makes this type of promotion stand out and the reason it grabs people's attention is that we make _**EVERYONE**_ a winner!

Right after we ran The Solution campaign for Matt Woelfel from Ground Round, we set up a March Madness promotion to drive people in during the NCAA games. Ground Round is more of a restaurant than a bar, but Matt's goal has been to make his bar busier, so we thought that doing a big-screen giveaway during March Madness would help sales in the bar.

Here's a look at the campaign we ran for him. I'll cover this from left to right of the image.

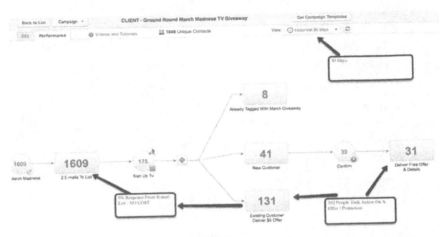

First, we sent two emails to his list. You can see from the image on the left that his customer list at this time was 1,609 people. These two emails explained the TV giveaway promotion, and how they could win. The call-to-action was to click a link in the email that would take them to another lead-capture page to sign up to win the TV.

Here is the lead-capture page that we took them to.

March Madness TV Giveaway

How would you like to win a 60" TV?

Sign up for a chance to win during our March Madness Promotion!

The first 50 people who sign up will be guaranteed winners of a free meal, a gift card, or other valuable prizes!

Rules: Must be 21 years of age to win. Must be present to win.

| First Name |
| Email |
| Birthday (xx-xx-xxxx) |

Submit

The 60" TV will be give away after the NCAA Men's Basketball Championship game on Monday April 4th.

Remember what I said in Section Two: A lead-capture page is a simple, one-page website that states the offer you are making and has a form that allows your prospect to enter their information.

We made everyone winners by telling them that if they signed up to win, they were guaranteed a free meal or a $5 gift card. Not everyone won the TV, but if they signed up to win the TV, _they'd win something._ All of this was explained in the email and Facebook ads so nobody was misled in anyway.

As you can see in the image of the campaign (page 125), a total of 175 people signed up to win the TV. If you look over to the right, you'll see a little square and three more, bigger rectangles branching off.

That little square is a "decision diamond" within our software. It makes a decision and tells the software where to place the customer. In this example it calculates whether or not the person who just signed up is on our current customer list or not.

If they were a brand new contact, they'd go into a "new customer" follow-up sequence that gave them a free meal. If they were an existing customer, they'd go into the "existing customer" $5 gift-card campaign. I do the free meal offer for new customers because in order to get new customers in the door, you need a more valuable offer. I would also talk to the new customers differently, just like I do within the "cheers" letter I covered in Section Two.

From the stats, you can see that 131 existing customers signed up to win. Forty-one brand new customers signed up to win. We ran a $50 ad on Facebook targeting men who had an interest in NCAA basketball and lived within 5 miles of Ground Round. It cost us a little over $1 per new lead to sign up.

If you do the math on the existing customers we targeted within the customer return path, it comes out to about a 9% response to this promotion. As I said before 5% to 10% response rates are pretty common. That's compared to the 1% or 0.05% when you target the masses through traditional media.

Here's a tip.

See that 39 in the circle?

Confirm

Anytime I'm running a lead-capture promotion, and we get a new lead in the system, we always send a follow up email, saying, *"Thanks for signing up, but for us to make sure you signed up for this, please click this link, and we can deliver your offer right away!"*

I do this because some people put in bad email addresses, thinking that they will be taken to a download page right way to get the offer. This process eliminates the bad email addresses. Once someone clicks that "confirm" link in the first email, a second email is sent to them right away with their offer, which has an expiration date tied to it based on the day they signed up.

The very top sequence, which says 8, represents the people who tried to sign up twice. They were put into a sequence that replied back, *"Sorry, you've already signed up once. If not, please respond back, so we can fix this issue."*

There will always be a few people who try to cheat the system or who maybe didn't think they completed the form. That's why we put these little security features in place.

Advanced Strategy

Creating urgency and scarcity is very important because people tend to forget about things when they live such busy lives. For every lead-capture promotion I run, I have a piece of software that creates a ***personalized*** expiration date for the offer ***based on the day the person signs up.***

In this example, customers had 10 days to use the offer. If someone signed up on March 1, the email that delivered their offer would tell them that it expires on March 11. If they signed up on the 5th, it would expire on the 15th.

To track these to ensure that people don't use multiple times, each person has their own unique ID number attached to the e-mail. We entered that ID number into our system, which tagged them when they used the offer. If they tried again, the system told the server or manager that they had already used it and on what date they did so.

The Follow-Up to the Big Giveaway

Within your follow-up emails (after people sign up), you need to tell them how they will win the big prize. I'll explain how I run this promotion on the day of the giveaway in order to make the most money, which is exactly what Matt followed.

1. We make everyone a winner in order to get the most sign-ups, and we give all of them a valuable offer that is tied to a 10-day expiration date. We make sure that this offer is ___NOT___ valid on the day we give away the big prize. In doing this, we are trying to get people in before the big day and the day of, thereby *increasing customer visits.*

2. Our second goal is to pack the house on the day of the promotion so each customer must be present to win. Everyone who comes in for the promotion receives a ticket

for a chance to win the big prize. In order to increase their chances of winning and to increase our average ticket value, for every item they buy, they get _another_ ticket.

At the end of the game, you draw the winner who then walks away with the TV.

3.   Matt got one of the liquor companies to partner with him on this. They gave him $500 to get the TV, so this promotion only cost him about $50 in Facebook ads to new and existing customers. Matt said he had 6 to 10 people in for the final game of March Madness in previous years, but this year he had 45 to 50 people! That's not bad for $50 in ad costs.

$10,000 Giveaway Promotion

If you gave people a fun and exciting way to win $10,000, do you think you'd get a crowd for it? Of course you would!

I'm going to show you the results of this promotion for Ground Round and a few other clients and explain how we ran it. Just keep in mind that you can take this promotional concept and use it in multiple ways throughout the year.

During the month of March, we ran a "Pot of Gold" promotion for St. Patrick's Day, where people were given the chance to win $10,000. We used a company called Interactive Promotions, which allowed you to buy insurance on the $10,000 game.

Interactive Promotions has a bunch of different promotions you can run to bring in big crowds. I use them several times per year. Great customer service. Their phone number is 888-882-5140 and their website is InteractivePromotions.com. Make sure you let them know you're a customer of Bar Restaurant Success. I send many clients their way.

Interactive Promotions sends your restaurant / bar three sets of games that have 20 security-sealed envelopes. Within those envelopes, there are three grand-prize winners. In order for someone to win one of the games, they must be the first to open all three grand-prize winners out of the 20 envelopes that you hang from the wall or ceiling.

The odds are in the house's favor, so to make each game last longer, you can allow customers to open seven to ten envelopes that have gift cards and other prizes printed on sheets of paper inside. These are not grand-prize winners, but even though they don't win the $10,000, they keep winning multiple prizes. It's still fun to play and exciting for everyone to watch.

How We Promoted This In The Customer Return Path

We ran this giveaway as another lead-capture promotion to engage with our current customer list and to build our list with new customers. We set it up in exactly the same way we did the flat-screen TV giveaway; we made everyone a winner. It was the same concept and the same strategy but a different type of promotion.

Here's an image of the results from Ground Round.

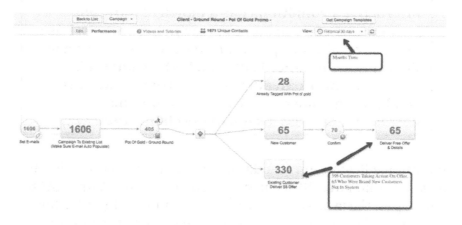

First we sent two emails to Matt's existing customer list, which was 1,606 people. Then we ran about $50 in Facebook ads to new customers in his area. We created ads that targeted specific demographics but **_EXCLUDED_** anyone who was on Matt's email list. This focused our marketing efforts on brand new customers, so we could build our list even more.

As you can see, 330 existing customers out of 1,606 took action—**about *20% of Matt's list***. Sixty-five brand new customers signed up. New customers got a free meal for signing up, just like the TV giveaway promotion, and existing customers got $5 gift cards.

Here's an example of the lead-capture page we used. When people clicked on the sign-up button, an opt-in form appeared to capture their names, email addresses, and birthdays.

How To Run This Promotion To Make The Most Profit

Of course you would want to send out a few email and text reminders to everyone who signed up a day or two before the promotion, letting them know the date and time and how they can win.

Because your bar/restaurant gets three different games, we set up the drawing of the winners to be every hour for three hours to make the excitement last as long as possible. We hang the envelopes from Interactive Promotions on the wall with a big pot of gold on the outside of the envelope and number them from 1 to 20.

To increase people's chances of getting picked for a chance to win, we do the same thing as the TV giveaway. For every item a customer buys, they get more tickets for a chance to be picked. If they are picked, they come up and choose three envelopes. If they don't pick the three grand-prize winners, we let them pick seven more envelopes with other prizes.

Think Outside The Box

There are multiple ways you can use this promotional concept all year round. One of the first "done for you" promotions I ever created and sold was to college bar owners, and it was based on this concept. We gave college girls a chance to win free boob job during Breast Cancer Awareness Month. The promotion and sign-up process was the same as I just mentioned, but if someone won, they had to spend that $10,000 with the sponsoring doctor to get the job done. The doctor paid for the $500 or so in insurance to promote the event.

The doctor received all the leads of the girls who signed up for chances to win. Then he followed up with his "Starving Crowd" of women who wanted boob jobs. Out of the few hundred women we got to sign up who didn't win the $10,000, I'm sure the doctor got a few new clients using other financing options.

I ran this promotion at my own bar, and it was a success. Lots of fun, nobody won though, *but I did upset a few older loyal female customers that never showed*. Think first about the promotion and concept you choose. This wasn't the perfect promotion for me to run, but I was young and wild at the time, and I didn't think about ALL of my customers. I thought about myself and the younger demographics. Lesson learned!

Profitable Birthday Campaigns

According to the National Restaurant Association®, 70% of adults visit a restaurant/bar on their own or someone else's birthdays. That's a HUGE number that can't be ignored and is exactly why you should have a birthday system in place.

I'll tell you how I set up my automated birthday systems within my customer return path to get the most birthday visits possible. Then I'll talk about the different types of birthday offers you can make.

How The System Works

Ten days before the customer's birthday, we send out a text message to their phone, saying, *"Hey, it's Bob from Bob's Restaurant. I just saw that you had a birthday coming up in a and I just sent you an e-mail with a birthday gift! Look for it now if you have a second! Enjoy!"*

I send an automated text first because 98.7% of people read their texts within 20 minutes of getting them, and only 20% to 25% of your emails will be opened on average. I send out the text to make sure the customer sees my message, which will encourage them to search for their gift in their email. That's just a *little secret to boost your conversions of birthday offers.*

Within the email I give the customer two choices: Gift A or Gift B. I tell them to pick one gift by clicking on one of the links.

Next they get taken to a thank-you page, which tells them to check their email for the gift they chose. We send the birthday gifts of some clients by mail. If we do that, we have a fulfillment list sent to the client's manager or direct-mail house with the contact's information and what to send them in the mail.

What To Use As Birthday Gifts

There are lots of things you can offer as birthday gifts, such as gift cards, free meals, percentages off tabs, percentages off a table of four or more people, free birthday cakes, a free party room, etc.

Look at what your competition is doing, and then think of how you can structure your offer to be more valuable, but in a way that still makes you the profit you need.

Run The Numbers

Let's say you have a list of 1,000 customers. If you divide that by 12 months, you get 80 customers a month, on average, who would be go through this automated system, wherein you contact them in a very personal way and offer them an amazing birthday offer.

If you can get 10% of those people to convert for your offer, eight people or groups are coming in for birthdays.

The problem with many birthday clubs and offers is that they are *boring*. You get a postcard saying, *"Happy birthday! Here's a free meal,"* or you get an email with a coupon attached. It's no different than anyone else's offer. Not many businesses send personalized text messages saying, *"Hey, I just sent you an email because I see your birthday is coming, and I've got two valuable gifts for you to choose from!"*

The little things make a big difference, especially when you're communicating on a personal level through your customers' personal communication channels that they use on a day-to-day basis. Don't hesitate to go the extra mile and stand out from your competitors.

Conclusion

I can give you another 50 different types of promotions that you can run within the customer return path, but I don't want to give you information overload. These types of promotions work best and bring in the most revenue for my clients.

Focus on one promotion, set a goal, and conquer it using the customer return path. I've given you the strategy to almost eliminate any risk of your promotion flopping. That strategy *should be used on a consistent basis.* Your customers will appreciate you for asking them and actually taking action on their input. It's a total game-changer!

In Section Four, I'll give you four simple blueprints to follow to add a minimum of $50,000 in sales over the next 12 months. I'll also reveal every step of my New Customer Attraction and Retention System that I implement in my bars and my clients' bars and restaurants. After that, I'll give you two fast-action plans to put my LRVO formula to work for you, on autopilot, whether you want to do this yourself or hire it out to someone local.

Section 4:
Your Step By Step Guide To Doubling Your Loyal Customers In The Fastest & Least Riskiest Way

Chapter 9:
My New Customer Attraction & Retention System & 4 Blueprints To Add $50,000 In Sales Or More In 12 Months

Right now I'm going to walk you step-by-step, through my process for building out, a fully automated system to attract and retain new customers.

In the members' area, you'll get a list of resources for everything you need to implement this automated system in your business. I didn't put all of the resources and pricing into this book because prices with CRM companies change, and I don't want what you're reading to be outdated.

To access your Members area, go to
www.BRSBookMember.com

List of Things You Need to Get Started

1. **CRM software**—This is what allows you to capture people's contact information and integrate with your web forms online. It allows you to send out automated marketing messages by email, text messages, and direct mail. There is a lot of CRM software out there, and most work great. In the Resources section of your Members area, you'll see who I recommend.
2. **Facebook ad account**—I always start with Facebook ads for driving traffic to our lead-capture pages because it's the most profitable PAID advertising that you can do right now to attract and retain new customers.
3. **Website**—I'm sure you already have a website, but if not, it's time to get one. You'll need a website, so you can create lead-capture pages to collect people's information for your offers.

4. **Implementer**—The last thing I want you to do is learn how to build websites and use marketing automation software. Stick to focusing on your business, your goals, and your customers' experiences. Outsource everything you don't want to do or that you're not an expert in. (I wish I would have taken that advice from day one!) You'll need to find someone local who builds websites and works with CRM software. As I said, I'll give you a very simple way to find this person in the fast-action plans I have for you.

My Step-by-Step, Automated, New Customer Attraction and Retention System That's Responsible for Creating the Highest-Grossing Online Promotions, With Zero Marketing Expenses, in The History of the Bar and Restaurant Industry...Revealed!

Remember, this follows the LRVO formula, and your ultimate goal is to attract the people with whom you want to do business. You want those people to hand over their information to you in exchange for a valuable offer to do business with you. I may sound like a broken record, but there's a reason for it. **These are the most profitable people to market to in the future. We focus on the lifetime value of the customer, not the first-time sale. The money is in the customer return path.**

Step 1: Drive Traffic & Get A Lead

The first thing you do is drive traffic from Facebook and Instagram to your lead-capture page, using video ads, image ads, and Facebook's lead ads. Some people react differently to different ads, so it's always good to test a variation. The people you want to target are those actively buying beer, wine, liquor, and meals at other bars and restaurants and who live within three miles of your business. These are your perfect customers.

> **Keep in mind, you can also get leads in house by using your staff to sign people up and add them to your automated system.**

If They Opt In & Say YES, I Want Your Offer

If they sign up for your offer, a few things magically happen. First, as soon as you get a new lead, we have a piece of software that integrates that contact with your Facebook custom audiences. I touched on this earlier in the book, but as a quick reminder, this piece of software builds a separate audience to market to in Facebook.

This means that if you ever want to **_ONLY_** market to people on Facebook who have given you their personal contact information, you can. You'll want to do that with all of the new promotions you run because these people are more profitable to market to then anyone else. If you want to run ads to **NEW** customers on Facebook and eliminate marketing to any of the existing customers on your list, you can **EXCLUDE** them in your targeting options when creating your ad.

Having this software automatically updates your Facebook custom audience a few times a day which will make life so much easier and more profitable.

The second thing that happens after they opt in is that they are taken to a thank-you page, saying, *"How would you like to get $60 in extra gift cards? If so, enter your phone number below."*

If they enter their phone number, they get a text within 60 seconds, saying, *"Hey Bob, thanks for signing up to BUSINESS NAME VIP text club. I'll be sending you a $5 off text coupon on the first of every month!"*

I'll explain more about this $60 in a second, but I want to cover this first! After people give you their phone number, they are taken to the final thank-you page, which is what I call a "share" page. This share page asks them to "share" your offer with their friends on Facebook.

Here is an image of a pretty simple share page.

They click on the blue share button, and a message pops up on **_THEIR_** Facebook page, saying, *"I just got (offer) from (business). Click this link to get one before they stop this promotion!"* There will also be the image of a gift card.

If people see this on their pages and click it, they will be taken to your lead-capture page to sign up! **This is a free way to build your list.**

Thank-You Page To Get Phone Number

The focus of the thank-you page is to get the customer's phone number, so you can send them broadcast text messages and automated text messages that are built into your marketing system.

How do they get their $60 in gift cards? On the first of every month, an automated text goes out to your customers, telling them that if they show this text, they get $5 off.

In order to get the best response, you add a five-day expiration date. For example, if they get the offer on the 1st of the month, it expires on the 6th.

Here's the cool part:

1. Each month they get the text, and it's automated.
2. Each month the expiration date changes to that given month, but it stays on the 6th.
3. You have a redemption code tied to each customer. When you enter that code into your system, it "tags" the customer in your system.
4. After the customer is tagged, an automated, but very personalized, email goes out 24 hours later from the owner, saying, *"Thanks for coming in! Hope everything went well. If you don't mind, would you rate your service?"*

Within this email there are two links. One says, *"We had a great time,"* and the other says, *"We didn't have such a great time."* If the customer clicks that they had a great time, an email goes to the owner, letting them know that that person, with all of their contact information attached to the e-mail, had a good time. If the customer clicks that did not have such a good time, an email is sent to the owner to give them that information; this email also includes all of their contact information.

With this second step of the sign-up process, you have:

1. Created a way to deliver <u>more value</u> to the customer
2. Created an <u>*automated*</u> way to get them <u>back in more often</u>
3. Created a way to be able to send them text promotions—<u>*another personal media format to use*</u> in the customer return path for future promotions
4. Created a way for the customer to refer your business and offer to all of their friends on Facebook, ***resulting in a bigger list of qualified customers at no expense to you***
5. **MOST IMPORTANT** - Created a way to get automated customer feedback—good or bad—from your customers – If there's bad feedback, you have the ***<u>easiest and most personalized way to find out what happened, show that you care, and win them over.</u>***

Whether you're an absent owner or not, this ***<u>customer feedback system is critical</u>*** to keeping you up-to-date on whether or not your staff is performing well. Ultimately, if a loyal customer is worth $5,000 a year to you, think of how much money this ONE THING could do for your business.

If They Click on Your Facebook Ad & Say "No, I <u>Don't</u> Want Your Offer!"

If a customer doesn't convert to a lead, you have at least "pixeled" them with your Facebook re-targeting pixel. Re-targeting occurs when you place a piece of code on your website that tracks all visitors. This "pixel" builds a list of all of those visitors in Facebook and other re-targeting platforms where you can re-market to those specific people.

144

Here's how to look at people who don't opt in the first time:

1. You can create ads that **ONLY** target people who hit your lead-capture page and **NOT** the thank-you page. These ads would focus on making those people the same offer again and _driving them back to your lead-capture page._ If you do this, **I suggest you only set those ads to hit those people for 3 more days.** If you do any more than that and they still haven't clicked over to get your initial offer, you're wasting money.

2. Maybe this offer wasn't exactly for them, but one of your future promotions, events, or specials will be. You can target all of these people with your other promotions. Remember, this list will be somewhat small; only a few thousand people. That means to create and run ads to these highly qualified people who showed some type of interest in your business and your offer won't cost you much money.

Your ROI will skyrocket because you're **not** marketing to the masses, but to those whom you know have expressed interest in your bar or restaurant. **_Don't give up on the disinterested people; _**_you can convert them into paying customers in the future with minimal investment._

Step 2: Confirm, Deliver, & Build Instant Trust & Credibility

If the person has opted in, you send them a confirmation email to make sure they gave you the right email address. As I said in Section Three, some people will sign up and give the wrong email address, thinking they will be taken directly to the download page.

The big downfall of an email list full of bad email addresses is that your delivery rate goes way down. Certain email providers see that and start sending some of your emails to spam. **It's not about the size of your list but the quality of your list and the relationship you have with it.**

The Confirmation Campaign

If a customer gave you a good email address, they will obviously open their email, and you will ask them to click the link within it to give you the right to send them the offer for which they signed up. This is also known as a "double opt-in."

What if they get sidetracked and don't check their email right away? You send a few follow up emails over five days that remind them to click the link to get the offer.

If they don't click the link after 3 follow-up emails, you place them in a campaign that deletes them 60 days later because all those e-mails do is hurt you in the future. Bad email addresses and people who are not serious about doing business with you are not good for your conversions!

New-Customer-To-Loyal-Customer Campaign: What Happens When They Click In The Confirmation Email

When a customer clicks the link to receive the lead-magnet offer, they receive your "Cheers Letter" by email, the one I mentioned in Section Two of the LRVO overview. This Cheers Letter is your first personal communication with your new lead, where you deliver your offer as promised and tell them who you are, what you stand for, and anything else you can say that represents you and your business in a good way AND that is the TRUTH!

Within this email, you create a personalized expiration date of 10 days for each lead that comes through. If someone signs up on November 1, their offer within the email will say it expires on November 11. If someone signs up on the 2nd, it will say it expires on the 12th!

You also add their contact ID number to this offer, so you can track redemptions, just like the text message. When you put the customer ID number into your system, the customer is "tagged" as having used this first offer, and an automated email from the owner goes out to them, saying, *"I saw you used your 50% off offer yesterday. I just wanted to find out how the service was. How was the food? Is there anything we can do better next time to serve you?"*

You make this email all about **THEM** and how you can better serve **THEM**. This builds instant trust and credibility, and it also blows the customer away because they ***NEVER*** get personalized follow-up messages from anyone else about how their experience was and what that business can do better to serve them next time!

Powerful, strategic, follow-up is what makes you stand out from everyone else. It's what starts these customers seeing you as genuine and gets them to **WANT** to do business with you even more!

Lead Magnet Reminder Campaign: What Happens If They Don't Come In Right Away To Redeem?

Our ultimate goal when it comes to marketing is getting a conversion; getting a customer to hand over their information, click a link, walk through your doors, etc. There's always a call-to-action that leads to some kind of goal/conversion.

If the customer doesn't come in within five days of getting the lead-magnet offer, you send out reminder emails to let them know that they have five days left until their offer expires. You send another email a few more days before it expires and a final one on the last day.

People will **NOT** get these reminder emails once they redeem because the system will stop the emails. The goal of this "reminder" campaign is to boost the response and get more people in your doors, taking advantage of your offer.

The Survey Campaign

As I stated in Section Two, three days after someone opts in to your lead magnet, you send them an email, asking them to fill out a short survey to find out how you can better serve them. You want to know what kind of food and drink specials they like, what types of promotions they like, and why they choose one bar or restaurant over another.

When people fill out this survey (We get about a 30% response.), their responses are sent to the owner, so he can start looking for patterns and understanding what his customers want. He's learning about his "Starving Crowd." Once he does this, he can run the A/B campaign for his next new promotion and find out which promotion has the biggest "Starving Crowd."

If you don't know what I mean by the "Starving Crowd," back up to the last few pages of Section Three, and you'll instantly find out why this is so important.

Birthday Campaign

The reason I always ask for a person's birthday on the first opt-in form is because I know how lucrative a birthday follow-up system can be. Every lead that you get should be placed into the birthday campaign I talked about in Section Three—big-money promotions.

Remember that it is really important to first send a person an automated text about 10 days before their birthday, telling them that you just sent them an email with a birthday gift.

Then, of course, make sure your email goes out right after the text. This way, you'll increase your conversions and get more people opting in to their birthday offers.

When you have a list of 1,000 customers who like you, trust you, and **WANT** to do business with you, it's not hard to get a 10% response rate. If you divide 1,000 customers by 12 months, that's 80 people per month, on average, getting your personalized, automated messages. I already gave you these numbers for this promotion in Section Three, but it's important to understand that this could be a very easy way to get eight to ten small birthday groups in your doors, with zero marketing expenses besides a few cents for the first text that goes out to them.

What Exactly Is Happening Right Now?

Before I dive into the $50,000 blueprint, let's get clear about what this system is doing on auto-pilot once it's set up. Once it's set up, it's set up forever, and you don't have to touch a thing.

If you want to crank it up, you spend more marketing dollars. If you want to turn it off, you stop running ads. You can also slowly build it with free-traffic strategies like having contests with among your staff regarding who can get the most opt-ins and use a promo code on the lead-capture page.

Ten Automated Ways That This System Builds You An Unstoppable Bar Or Restaurant Business

1. You are targeting your most profitable prospects on the two largest social media platforms, Facebook and Instagram, at a budget you're comfortable with. I typically advise starting with $200 per week for the first 2 weeks, but every market is different. It really boils down to the size of the audience you're targeting and how driven you are to scale your business fast!

   I'm sure you've heard that *"Your investment into your business is relative to your return."* Meaning that if you spend $1 on advertising, you won't get much back, if anything. If you spend $500, your opportunity is much higher.

2. You are building a re-targeting list from everyone who hits your webpage from your paid ads and free traffic from the share page. You can use this re-targeting list in the future for other promotions. This gives you a pretty high ROI on your marketing dollars because you are focusing ONLY on those people who express interest in your business rather than targeting a bunch of random people who may have never heard of you before.

3. You are building your Facebook custom audience list on autopilot based on every lead that you get because your marketing system automatically updates your list every six hours.

4. You are getting a good percentage of your leads to refer your lead-magnet offer page and business to their friends on Facebook—*for free*—from the share page

5. You are building your most valuable asset, your customer list, which allows you to send persuasive marketing messages to customers in the future by email and text, boosting your sales.

6. You are building instant trust and credibility with your customers thanks to the customer follow-up system. You have a better understanding of how your staff and business are performing for your customers. This is like having a spy in your business 24/7, letting you know what's going on when you're not looking.

7. You are getting customers in the door with urgency related to your marketing message. This increases the conversions of people walking in the door. You have automated follow-up messages that remind them that their offers are about to expire. Once they redeem their offers, these reminders get shut off automatically.

8. You are finding out some of the most valuable and profitable information you could ever get your hands on from the automated surveys. Your potential customers are telling you what they WANT, what they will come in and spend money on. You're learning exactly what you need to offer to your "Starving Crowd" in the future to create big days with minimal risk to your marketing dollars.

9. You are building an automated way to get as many people in the door for their birthdays.

10. **MOST IMPORTANT** You are building a relationship with your customers and making your brand stand out in the most positive and powerful way.

Step 3: Add $50,000 To Your Sales In 12 Months

As I stated earlier in the book, marketing is a numbers game. It's all about mathematics. You spend x, and you get back y. You could get a positive return or a negative return, but the truth is, ***there's always an average response rate when it comes to marketing, and it's important to know yours with each media you use in the customer return path.***

You send out 1,000 emails. A certain percentage of people open them, and a certain percentage of those people take the action you're asking of them. You send out direct mail, and you have a percentage of people that respond to your offer.

One **VERY** important lesson I learned and that I keep reminding myself of in everything I do is: Focus with **THE END IN MIND**. What is your goal? What is the outcome that you're looking for? Once you know, start working backwards before you start moving forwards! It may sound strange, but you'll see what I mean.

Right now, we want to add a minimum of $50,000 in additional sales to our business over the next 12 months, using this marketing and promotional system. That's the goal. Now we need to figure out how we're going to make that happen. The good thing is, there are several ways. What's important for you to figure out is which way or ways fit your business model.

As I've stated 100 times by now, the new customer attraction and retention system that I use myself, and for my clients follows the LRVO formula, which implements the three ways to grow any business: Get more customers, increase the average check, increase the amount of frequent visits. So let's dive in on how to do that with 4 different blueprints!

Loyal Customer Blueprint #1

Getting more customers starts with getting more leads to opt in for your lead-magnet offer and turning them into loyal customers through the follow-up marketing system.

Let's say you get 1,000 leads from your Facebook and Instagram ads and from the "Share" page that puts your offer in front of thousands of others for free.

If you can turn 5% of those leads over the course of 12 months into loyal customers who spend $100 per week with you, that's 50 more loyal customers, which is $52,000 in extra sales per year.

If you turn 2.5% of leads into $200-per-week customers, you reach the same goal.

If you turn 5% into $200-per-week customers, that's $104,000 in additional sales.

If you turn 10% of the 1,000 leads—100 customers—into $100-per-week customers, that's $520,000 in additional sales.

Here's what's important about blueprint #1: It's not hard to build a list of 1,000 people or get 300 to 500 new or past customers walking through your doors with a valuable offer that beats out your competition. The hard part is making sure your staff provides the best experience possible. If you do a great job at that, converting 5% of 1,000 people should be very easy for you.

If you feel this is an area in which your business and management can improve, I have created ways for you to get feedback, build trust, and build relationships on autopilot, in case an issue arises during a customer's visit. However, keep focusing on improving systems to hire the best employee's for your business and training systems that keep your staff improving. It's well worth the time and investment when you think about these numbers.

Customer Return Path Blueprint #2

Assuming you have your list built, the second way to grow your business is to get customers to come back in the door more often.

Let's say with a customer list of a 1,000 people, you get 5%— 50 people—to come back for just 1 extra visit per week, and they spend an extra $20 with you. That's an extra $1,000 in sales per week. Multiplied by 52 weeks, that equals $52,000. If you have a list of 2,000 people, that would be $104,000.

A bigger list **_doesn't_** mean more work. It means more people you can serve and benefit from with the same amount of time and effort as a 1,000-person list. Again, this is why I run at least four lead-capture campaigns throughout the year.

More leads into LRVO formula = more customers = equals more sales & profits = happier life

Plus more happy employees who love their job and the income it provides = more efficient business operation

---

How do you get customers coming back more often? By using the customer return path and your email, text, re-targeting, and direct mail lists to deliver valuable offers that benefit your customers, while at the same time building better relationships with them.

How Mark Added $50,000 In Sales Within 6 Months

A past client of mine, Mark Bares from Merril, WI, owns a bowling center. He wanted to increase his bar business because he didn't want to only be known as a bowling center. I helped Mark through each step of the LRVO formula and built him a list of 900 people in a matter of 2.5 months. **Each month we used the customer return path and sent out a monthly offer by direct mail. Mark got an average 18% response rate from his monthly mailers.**

That's HUGE!

Normal response to a cold list of prospects is 1% to 2%, if you're lucky. The only way to get results like Mark's is to market to people who gave you their information and with whom you've built relationships. Mark said that within 6 months, he's added nearly $50,000 in sales to his business by applying this LRVO formula.

The Truth Is...

When you follow what I say about "relationship"-based marketing and you talk to your customers in a conversational tone within your marketing messages, letting them know what's going on in the business and in your life, you'll see Blueprint #2 be quite easy to accomplish.

People do business with people whom they like and trust. That's the major thing that sets me apart from all of my competitors. I focus on building value, trust, and relationships through my marketing in a way that connects me to my new and existing customers. _**You can do the same thing**_ with everything I've taught you in this book.

Big Ticket Blueprint #3

The third way to grow any type of business is to get your customers to spend more money when they come in. Think about how you can create "big-ticket" offers, such as party packages and fundraiser packages that bring in 30 to 50 people who spend an average of $20. Better yet, aim for bigger groups of 75 to 100 or more.

If you book parties and events, you know your average sales per party or event, and you know how profitable they can be. If you had a list of 1,000 people, and you could get 5% to take you up on the big-money promotion I talked about in Section Three (The Solution), that's 50 people booking parties at your business. If you had a list of 2,000 people, that would be 100 people booking parties. Matt from Ground Round booked 122 parties with a list a little over 1,600 people!

It may sound insane, but I've already shown you three case studies in Section Three that all had around a 5% response rate to this offer and that did between $10,000 and $60,000 in sales from just one promotion. They didn't even tie in birthday parties over the course of 12 months.

Imagine if you ran two to three party-booking promotions over the course of a year, and you could get a 2.5% to 5% response rate from just email, with a list of only 1,000 people. You would have zero marketing costs!

LRVO Blueprint #4

If you follow the five-step LRVO formula and my new customer attraction and retention system, and you stay in consistent communication with your customers, ***you're following Blueprint #4.***

If I told you that you can increase your sales by 33.1% if you focus on it for 5 hours per week, would you believe me?

If you can increase the average number of customers you have, the average transaction size, and the average amount they spend by just 10%, you'll expand your sales by 33.1%!

I want you to plug your own numbers into this, but let's say you have 500 customers, on average, who come in every month. They spend an average of $20, and they come in just once a week or 4 times per month. What would happen if you could increase each of those numbers by 10%, using the LRVO formula? Let's look at this example for a small bar or restaurant.

500 customers x $20 x 4 visits per month = $40,000 per month

500 customers x 10% increase = 550 customers per month
$20 spent (average) x 10% increase = $22
4-time average visit per month x 10% increase = 4.4

550 x $22 x 4.4 = $53,240 per month

That's a $13,240 difference in sales per month, or $158,880 per year, just by increasing 10% to each of the three ways it takes to grow your business. The good news is, when you follow the LRVO formula and use the customer return path, this is what happens to your business because this is what LRVO is all about.

Conclusion

Based on what I just laid out and the case studies you've read within this book, you know this works.

The four blueprints I gave you are pretty simple formulas. To reach those kinds of numbers, you just have to think with the end in mind—getting 1,000 leads into your marketing system. From there, focus on turning 2.5% to 5% of those leads into loyal customers.

This works for any bar, any restaurant, any pizza shop, in any part of the world, as long as you can remember that *you are in the business of creating great experiences for your customers.* This applies not only in-house but *through your "relationship"-based marketing messages.*

"But Nick, I don't know all this tech/website craziness you're talking about! I love what you're saying, but this shit sounds hard!"

Sounds hard? *That's business.* That's life! There's no such thing as easy money or an easy life in the bar/restaurant business. If you want to be the best, and if you want to make a lot of money, that takes **hard work and dedication.**

I didn't understand all of this marketing automation stuff when I first started doing this in my first bar. I know exactly how you feel. Luckily, I was coached on what to do and how to hire it out by my marketing coach, Dave.

I'm doing the same for you. This chapter specifically is designed to coach you. I gave you the exact, step-by-step formula of how my new customer attraction and retention system works. *You know exactly what needs to happen, how it works, and why it works.*

Now you need to find someone who can put this to work for you. Let's dive into two fast-action plans to implement this because *without action, nothing will change for you.*

If you're ready for change, if you're hungry to be the best, if you're willing to step out of your comfort zone, then move on to the next chapter, where I give you the steps you need to take to start outsmarting your competition and building your brand and sales in the most powerful and profitable way.

Chapter 10:

2 Fast Action Plans To $50,000 Or More In Sales

Right now you should feel proud of yourself. You've made it this far into some pretty intense, high-level internet marketing strategies and concepts. You've made it through understanding the psychology of what gets people to take action and the 5 key ingredients you need in all your marketing messages to get the highest ROI. This shows you're hungry and motivated. This shows you can out beat procrastination! You're one of the few, so give yourself a hand! ***Now it's time to take one more small step to reach your goals.***

Here's one of my favorite quotes by Albert Einstein - *"You have to learn the rules of the game. And then you have to play better than anyone else."*

When it comes to attracting new customers and turning them into loyal customers and out-beating your competition, *you've learned the rules of the LRVO formula to make that happen.* When it comes to your competition, all you have to do is apply that formula to your business and **you'll be playing 10 times better than everyone else!**

Here Are 2 Fast Action Plans To Start Playing!

Action Plan #1: Hire Local

Find a website developer in your local area. Post a message on Facebook that you're looking for someone who can build a website. You'll get messages from 10 to 20 people within 60 minutes.

Step 1: Start the Process

Here's exactly what I want you to post on your Facebook page: *"I'm looking for someone who knows how to build websites using WordPress and can integrate an autoresponder system into my website. If you know someone, please have them inbox me. Don't put a message in this post; send me a private Facebook message, or I will not respond. If you know someone, please tag them. I appreciate your help!"*

WordPress is one of the most common themes to build websites, and there's a ton of drag-and-drop site builders that are WordPress-compatible. Auto responder system is the CRM software I referred to earlier.

The reason you should ask people on Facebook to send you private responses is to <u>see *who actually follows directions*</u>. If someone wants to work with you, but they can't follow one simple direction and they just reply to the post, you'll be doomed if you work with that person! Always qualify the people you want to work with!

Step 2: Why You?

Now that you're getting responses, I want you to respond to those with, *"Thanks for reaching out. I've had about 20 responses. Crazy! I'm overwhelmed reaching back out to everyone. (Name), can you tell me why I should choose you over everyone else?"*

If they can't give you a good enough answer, they are out. The ones who grab your attention are the key players you want to focus on working with.

Step 3: Qualify and Deliver the Details

Because I'm a HUGE believer in valuing your time, I've done something small, but **_very useful for you_**: I've taken my step-by-step overview of my new customer attraction and retention game plan and created a downloadable file for it in the Members area! When you have three to five key players in mind to work with, all you need to do is reply back to them and say, *"Read this document. It'll take you five minutes. This is exactly what I need. Please respond, and let me know if this is something you can do, and then let's jump on the phone and see if we can work together!"*

I guarantee you'll find people who can do this for you. There are downfalls to this, just as there are to everything else in life.

These are the questions you need to ask a candidate once you have someone in mind:

- Are they going to write all of the emails out for you? More importantly, do they know how to write persuasive marketing messages that get your customers to take action while building trust and credibility at the same time?
- How long will it take for them to get this done?
- Are they able to integrate all of your leads into Facebook custom audiences?
- Can they set up re-targeting for you and show you how to use it?
- Do they understand the five key ingredients to successful ads – if not, you don't want them writing your e-mail copy?
- Do they have happy, satisfied clients to back up their work that is similar to this type of system?
- What's it going to cost?

My advice is to hire the person who says they can do most or all of this, but ask them to show you and prove it. Get some testimonials from other clients for whom they've done similar things.

Action Plan #2:

Let My Team and I Do All the Work, Customized to Your Brand, Within Five Business Days, and Let Me Personally Coach You Each Month to Create Big Paydays in Your Business

Action Plan #2 is designed specifically for the busy owner who wants the fastest shortcut to getting a new customer attraction and retention system built for them.

If you don't want to write your own emails, search for the right person to set all this up for you, or go through the trial and error of making it all work with your local hire, then this might be for you.

If you're looking for personal coaching by me that will boost your productivity, allow me to personally help you each month with different promotional ideas, creating persuasive emails, and ultimately _take any guesswork out of knowing how to mine peak profit from your system_, then this might be for you.

Go to **www.LoyalLeads.net** to get more information.

On this page, you'll also discover a revolutionary piece of software that we've just recently added to our marketing system and that I believe every successful bar/restaurant owner will have working in their business within the next two years. If I'm wrong, I'll be shocked. It's a total game-changer! I didn't talk about it within this book, and you'll know why when you visit **www.LoyalLeads.net**.

Conclusion

I hope you received 100 times more value than what you invested into this book. It was my goal to give you everything I've got and to make this book the bar/restaurant owner's go-to guide for taking your marketing, promotions, and business to the next level with the least amount of effort and risk.

As I said in the first chapter, don't just read through this book one time. Re-read it multiple times. Memorize the LRVO formula. Mark up this book with notes and stars. Memorize the five key ingredients to successful ads that I gave you. By doing so, you'll have the ultimate advantage over your competition and the fastest way to build a powerful brand.

Thank you for reading, and I wish you much success,

Nick Fosberg

Want To Contact Nick For Private Coaching & Consulting?

Best way to reach out to Nick is by e-mail. You can e-mail him at **Nick@BarRestaurantSuccess.com**